S0-ACC-007

I'm turning on my PC, Now What?!™

by Matthew James

SILVER LINING BOOKS

NEW YORK

Copyright © 2000, 2001, 2002 Silver Lining Books
ISBN 0-7607-3254-x

All rights reserved. No part of this book may be reproduced or transmitted in any form or by any electronic or mechanical means, including information storage and retrieval systems, without permission in writing with the exception of brief passages used in a critical article or review.

First Edition 2000
Fourth Edition 2002

For information address:
Silver Lining Books
122 Fifth Avenue
New York, NY 10011

Printed and Bound in the United States of America

Other titles in the Now What?!™ series:

I'm turning on my iMac, Now What?!
I'm in the Wine Store, Now What?!
I'm in the Kitchen, Now What?!
I need to get in Shape, Now What?!
I need a Job, Now What?!
I haven't saved a Dime, Now What?!
I'm on the Internet, Now What?!
I'm Retiring, Now What?!
I just bought a Digital Camera, Now What?!
I'm getting Married, Now What?!
I've got a Grill, Now What?!
I have to give a Presentation, Now What?!

introduction

The look on Karen Cohen's face was one of sheer horror. There directly in front of her was her new computer, plugged in and ready to go. All she had to do was push the On button. No shrinking violet, Karen pushed it, ready to take on this new world. Except the book she was using was less than helpful. There were a lot of techie words she had never heard of, weird diagrams that made no sense, solutions to problems she didn't know she even had. "Can't someone write a computer book in English?" she said with a sigh. "All I want to do is e-mail Elizabeth and JB, maybe write a letter. Why is that so hard?"

Why indeed. Maybe because most computer books are written by experts who have long forgotten what it was like to be a newbie (that's techspeak for the new computer user). We haven't forgotten. We recall all too clearly how anxious it feels to go online for the first time, or scan your first photo. In **I'm turning on my PC, Now What?!** we walk you through each new thing, spread by spread. No jargon, no excruciating details. We promise fun, smart, painless understanding. No more horror-struck looks. So turn on your computer and see how easy it can be.

Barb Chintz

Editorial Director, the *Now What ?!*™ series

table of contents

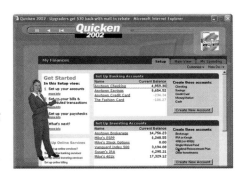

Starting

1

With your computer at hand,
you are now a part of the brave new world!
Now what? Connecting it and turning it on.
Oh, yes, and learning how to use the mouse
and what all those little things on the screen do.
It's all here in the first chapter. So relax.
The brave new world is just a page away.

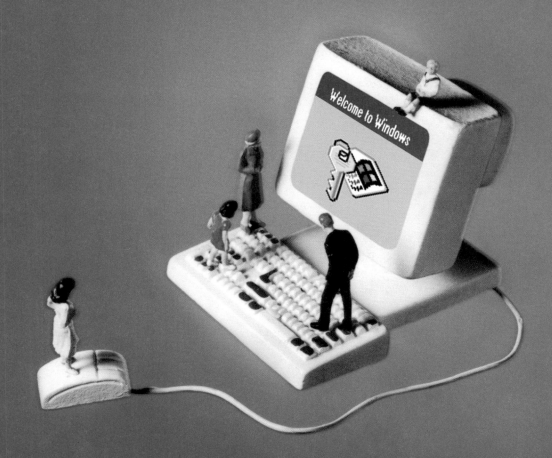

Welcome to Windows

setting up

Ready to venture out onto the high-tech seas?

Congratulations! You've done it. You bought a computer. But there it sits, waiting to be unpacked, and even worse, waiting to be put together. Chances are you're feeling a little anxious that you'll never get all the parts connected right. Or worse, connect them and then blow the computer up. Fear not—nearly all computers come with easy-to-follow instructions, and no one has ever blown one up.

That said, if you find yourself overwhelmed by all the cables and plastic boxes, stop. Take a deep breath. Exhale. Go to your phone and start dialing around for a "techie," someone who knows how to do this and even enjoys it. Call your local computer store and ask them if they have someone who sets up computers. They usually have a repository of freelance techies who charge by the hour. Or call your friends with teenage children and ask if their offspring could set up your computer for you.

Help is only a phone call away. Try ringing up a friendly teenager. This generation grew up with computers and actually thinks it's fun to put them together.

STEP BY STEP: UNPACKING

1. Unpack the cardboard boxes. You should have a **monitor** (looks like a TV), **tower** (plastic or metal box that stands and houses the computer's innards; older computer models have **consoles** instead of towers, and monitors typically rest on top of them), a **keyboard** (a tray of typewriter keys and other buttons), a **mouse** (plastic device the size of a bar of soap). And, often, a pair of audio speakers. You will also find **computer cables** (plastic-covered cords; some have funny-looking plugs; others have the standard three prongs).

2. Save the packing boxes in case you need to ship something back.

3. Put the console or tower near the monitor. Place the audio speakers on either side of the monitor.

4. If your computer came with a printer, place it near the console or tower; then wait until later to set it up. (See page 30.)

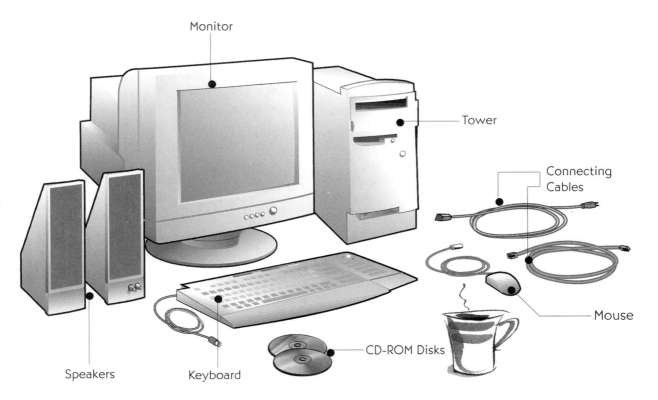

Monitor

Tower

Connecting
Cables

Mouse

Speakers

Keyboard

CD-ROM Disks

plugging in

You've boldly gone and taken it out of the box. Now what?!

Okay, you say, you want to try. Fine. It should take less than an hour or up to 45 days, depending on your frame of mind. The goal is to connect all the **hardware** (the big plastic and metal boxes) with the **computer cables** (plastic-covered cords). Once that is done, you will connect the **peripheral** hardware (keyboard, audio speakers). Below you'll see the various types of cables you will be dealing with. You can tell them apart by their ends. Some of these ends will fit into various **ports**, or openings, of your computer; others will plug into electrical sockets. See the following page to get an idea about how they typically connect. (Note: Every computer manufacturer has its own ways to go about it, so get the instruction book out.)

SURGE PROTECTORS

The electrical power in your house doesn't stay at a constant 110 volts. If someone turns on air conditioners or vacuum clean-

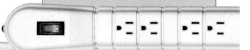

ers in another room, the power can spike up high throughout your house. Lightning storms can do the same. Power surges like these can wreak havoc with the delicate insides of a computer. So it's a good idea to plug your computer's power cables into a special kind of power strip called a surge protector. Surge protectors have four or five power outlets like regular power strips, but they contain special gizmos to take the sting out of a power surge. You can get them at any local computer or office supply store for $15 or less.

Monitor cable connects the monitor to the tower or console. Sometimes one end of the cables is **hardwired** (permanently attached to the monitor). You just need to attach the other end to the tower or console.

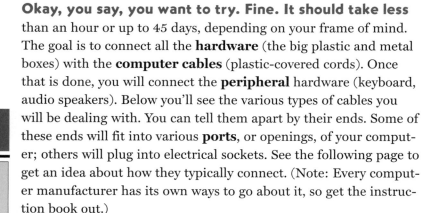

A typical power plug that connects the tower or console to your electrical outlet.

To connect your computer tower or console to your mouse, keyboard, and printer, you will be provided with either USB cables (1), which have flat, square ends, or serial cables (2), which have round ends containing prongs.

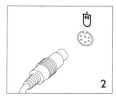

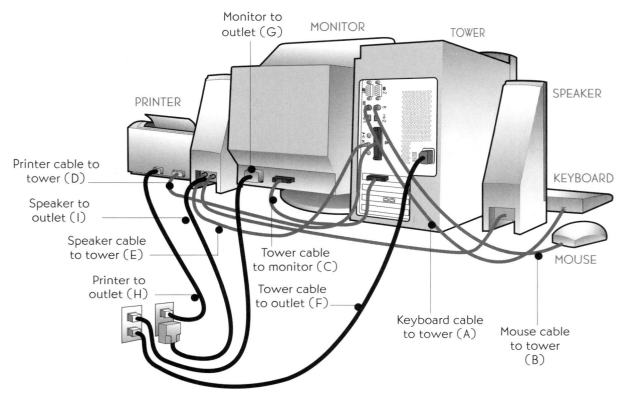

Monitor to outlet (G)

MONITOR

TOWER

SPEAKER

PRINTER

KEYBOARD

Printer cable to tower (D)

Speaker to outlet (I)

Speaker cable to tower (E)

Tower cable to monitor (C)

MOUSE

Printer to outlet (H)

Tower cable to outlet (F)

Keyboard cable to tower (A)

Mouse cable to tower (B)

S TEP BY STEP: PLUGGING IN

1. First, get out your computer instruction book. Now breathe. All you're going to do is find all the cables that have funny looking plugs and insert them into matching holes, or ports, in the back of the computer.

- the keyboard to the console or tower (A)
- the mouse to the console or tower (B)
- the monitor to the console or tower (C)
- the printer to the console or tower (D)
- the speakers to the console or tower (E)

2. Once those are connected, find the standard electrical wires and plug those into your nearby electrical wall outlet or surge protector (see page 10).

- console or tower to outlet (F)
- monitor to outlet (G)
- printer to outlet (H)
- speaker to outlet (I)

3. If you have a printer, wait and set it up later.
(See pages 28–29 for help plugging in your printer.)

getting comfortable

The smart, ergonomic way to sit pretty.

Whether you purchased a computer workstation or cleared off an old desk, you'll be fine. What you want is a sturdy surface with room for your keyboard and mouse. The chair needs to be high enough so your arms are bent at a 90-degree angle at the elbow when your hands are on the keyboard.

You will want a good lamp or overhead light to keep your eyes happy while looking at the monitor. If your computer is in a room with a large window, make sure that your desk is set up in such a way that you don't get a glare from the sun or are looking at the monitor with the sun in the background—each of these situations can make your eyes very tired and irritated.

Keep your eyes level with the top of the monitor. If the monitor is too low, prop it up with some of those coffee-table books you never read. If it is too high, sit on pillows.

Have your arms bent at a 90-degree angle at the elbow when your hands are on the keyboard (without bending your wrists).

Place your feet flat on the floor—no dangling. Better still, put your feet on a footrest under your desk to reduce lower-back stress. The footrest should be about 5 to 6 inches high.

HAT IF

You already have a good chair, and need a desk?

A card table will do if it's sturdy enough. Or pick up a second-hand desk at a thrift store. All you need is a flat surface that has enough room to hold your monitor and keyboard. The tower can be on the floor. Or you can buy a computer desk with a built-in keyboard tray.

You have the desk, but no chair?

Measure from the middle of your monitor on the desk to the floor. This will give you a good idea of the proper eye level when sitting in the chair. Then buy a chair that puts your eyes at that level when sitting.

You have an overhead light and it's casting too much glare?

Kill the overhead light and put a lamp beside your computer monitor so the light shines on your work area. If that still doesn't do it, you can buy an antiglare filter at your local computer store. This filter fits right over your monitor screen, acting like sunglasses.

You can't find the control buttons on your monitor?

Some of the more recent monitors have such slick designs that you can't find the control buttons to adjust your monitor's light and tone. (Older models have nice handy knobs.) Don't panic. The buttons are there, just hidden behind a pullout panel. Look for what looks like a crack in the plastic at the bottom of the monitor and pop it open. Behind it should lie your control buttons.

CARPAL TUNNEL SYNDROME

You've probably heard of it, and you definitely don't want to get it. Carpal tunnel syndrome is a condition often caused by repetitive activities done improperly, such as typing with your fingers above your wrists. Symptoms of carpal tunnel syndrome are numbness, tingling, or a sharp, shooting pain in your hand. To avoid this problem, make sure you type with your hands in a straight line with your forearms, not bent up or down. And try to give your hands frequent breaks. Stop every 15 minutes and rest your hands for a bit.

turning it on

This is Houston calling. Are you ready for liftoff?

You have all your computer cables connected, and the computer is plugged in. Now what? Push the **On** button located on the front of the console or tower. There's often a button underneath the On/Off button called the **Reset** button. Ignore it for now.

Okay, still breathing? The whirring noises you hear mean your computer is booting up (techspeak for when a computer starts up). You'll see some words whiz past. You'll see some images swoosh by. You may see the name of your computer's manufacturer. And you'll see the logo for Microsoft Windows. Windows is what techies call the **operating system**, the software that's in charge of your new PC. More on that on page 20. Next you will see an image of a little hourglass. This is Windows' quaint way of letting you know it's working—and that you'll need to wait. It will vanish when the computer's ready for you.

When the noises stop, you can start. Here's where it can get tricky. If your computer is brand-new, you will be asked to register it. See pages 16–17 for more details. If yours is a used computer, chances are it's been registered, so you bypass registration and immediately see the **desktop**—a screen (usually blue) with little symbols on it.

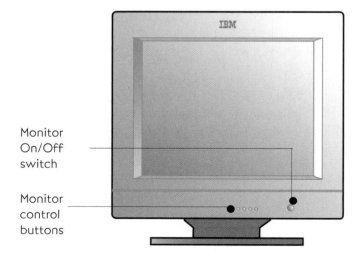

Monitor
On/Off
switch

Monitor
control
buttons

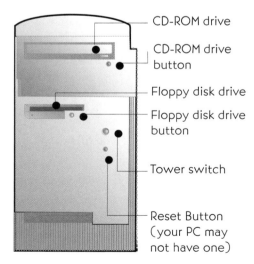

CD-ROM drive

CD-ROM drive
button

Floppy disk drive

Floppy disk drive
button

Tower switch

Reset Button
(your PC may
not have one)

WHAT IF

Your computer doesn't turn on?

If your computer is connected to a surge protector, make sure it's on. Next check the power outlet; test it with a lamp to make sure it's working. Now check your computer cables—unplug all the power cables, then re-plug them all and try again. Make sure the monitor button is on. Check the back of the computer's tower or console for a master power switch (some computers have them, some don't) and make sure it's on.

Your computer is making noises, but your monitor stays black?

Check that your monitor button is on and the cables are firmly connect-ed. Look at the monitor control buttons—they are the knobs directly underneath the screen. Find the brightness button and turn it. If the brightness button is turned all the way down, the screen will appear black.

FIRST PERSON DISASTER

Don't Take It Personally

My husband gave me a computer for my birth-day and I was thrilled, but also nervous about setting it up. The computer boxes sat in the guest room for the longest time. Finally, I got up the nerve and hooked it up like the instruc-tion book said. Then I pushed the 'on' button and nothing happened. I unplugged every-thing and hooked it up again. Still nothing. Now I was getting upset. I called the computer store and asked them what to do. They asked if I was sure the outlet worked. Of course it worked. The clock was plugged into the same outlet and it was working. They told me to keep checking the wiring. I did. Nothing hap-pened. I was sure it was me.

That evening my husband thought he'd give it a go and when he turned it on, it worked. What did he do differently? Nothing that I could see. Then it dawned on me, literal-ly. He'd turned on the light switch when he entered the room. The light didn't go on, but the computer did . . . because I had plugged it into the top socket, which was controlled by the wall light switch. We've since plugged the computer into a different outlet and it's been working just fine. I've learned not to take any-thing a computer does personally. Just keep trying and eventually you'll find the answer.

Jesse K., Nyack, New York

logging on

*Computers like
to serve only
one master*

Great, you've turned on your computer. Now what?

Well, the first time you run your computer, you'll be asked a few questions so that Windows (the software in charge of your computer, the **operating system**, remember?) can set everything up for you. One of the most important questions it will ask is whether more than one person will be using this computer. If so, you can type in the names of each person, so that when Windows starts up again, they can "sign in" by clicking on their name. This is called **logging on**, and the names of each person are called **user names**. You can also add a password so that nobody else who uses your computer can see your documents. If all this sounds a bit too much, you don't want to set up different user names and log-ins, just type in your own name and leave it at that.

Oh, and the first time out, your computer will most likely ask you to register your computer with the manufacturer—and maybe also with Microsoft (which makes Windows XP). You don't have to do this—you can just click the Cancel button—but it can help later on if you ever need to call the computer maker for technical support. You'll need to fill out your name and address and some other details in a form on the screen. What happens to this information? Nothing, unless you are connected to the Internet (see pages 58–60). If you are connected, you will be asked if you want to send your registration info to the company that manufactured your computer or software. Click yes or no as you wish.

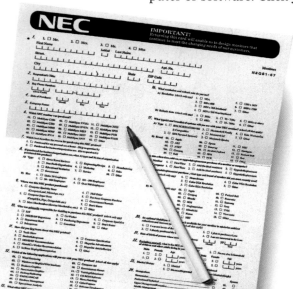

Nearly all modern appliances come with registration and warranty cards that most of us ignore. Your computer is no exception, except that its registration card pops up on the computer screen, making it harder to ignore.

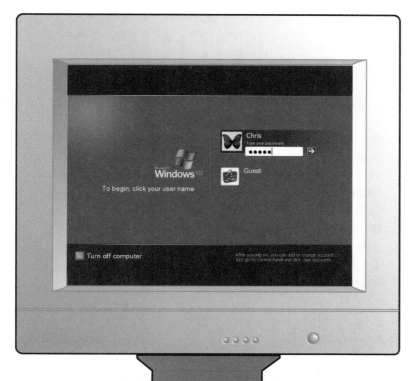

Logging on to Windows XP usually means clicking on your name in the list and maybe typing in a password. You don't have to set up lots of different user names or use passwords if you're the only person who uses the computer.

STEP BY STEP: LOGGING ON

If Windows XP is configured for more than one user, you'll stop at a screen like the one above until you have logged in. Here's how to do it:

1. With the left button on your mouse (the one under your pointing finger), click on your user name in the list. If you don't have a user name on this computer, click on the Guest link instead.

2. If there's a password associated with your user name, an empty box will appear next to it. Enter your password in it. Each character will appear as a big black dot, so if Agent Maxwell Smart is peeking over your shoulder, he can't read your password.

3. Click on the arrow next to your password box.

4. You'll see a new screen appear telling you your settings (your private files, among other things) are being loaded.

By golly, you did it! You've turned on your computer and launched Windows XP. Congratulations!

using the mouse

*Getting
handy with
your hands*

Fantastic. The computer is raring to go, and you're looking at all the little symbols on the screen. What now? Well, take another deep breath, because before you can do anything, you need to learn a wee bit about using something called a **mouse**. This clever little device serves both to move you around your computer screen and to activate commands. It's a bit like a car's stick shift in that it puts your computer into gear. Ready to drive? Okay, start moving the mouse. See that black or white arrow? It's called the **mouse pointer**. Move the mouse around and see how the pointer goes all around the screen: up, down, left, right, and diagonally.

Your mouse will most likely have two buttons (some have three). The *left* button is the one you'll click most often. When you **click** on an object it becomes "selected," but nothing actually happens. To make something happen, you will need to click twice—quickly. That's called a **double-click**.

Clicking on the button on the *right* side of the mouse is called a **right-click**. You use it when you are doing advanced computing; ignore it.

Left button

Right button

The mouse operates best on a mouse pad, typically a 5x7-inch rubber pad. Naturally, a mouse pad does not come with your new computer, so you have to buy one at your local computer or stationery supply store. Do you really need one? Yes. The rubber pad lets the mouse move more easily. If you don't have a pad, okay. Your desk surface will do in a pinch.

Ask the experts

What is an icon?

See those funny-looking pictures or symbols with one or two words under them? They are called icons. They are pictorial symbols showing the various functions and parts of your software. If you double-click on them, they will "open."

What is a screen tip?

If you move the mouse pointer over an icon and leave it there for a couple seconds without clicking, you will see a brief written description of that particular item, which is called a screen tip. These are useful if you want to know what an icon is for without actually clicking on it.

CLICK AND DRAG

Another action that you will be asked to perform with the mouse is called a click and drag. This requires you to move the mouse pointer over an object on-screen, click and hold down the left mouse button, then move or drag the mouse while continuing to hold down the left button. This allows you to move items on your screen to different locations.

Your mouse is an ingenious combination of a car's steering wheel and gearshift. Like a steering wheel, your mouse lets you zoom all around your desktop. And when you click on the mouse's buttons, it's just like putting your computer in gear.

your Windows desktop

What you see here is the Windows XP desktop. It's the latest in a long line of Microsoft Windows software, and it's different in many ways from its predecessors. But like older versions of Windows, it has a cluster of little pictures called icons along the left side. These are more than just pretty pictures. They are the "buttons" you click on to do all the wonderful things XP can do. You click on one of these to do pretty much everything on your computer. Here are the icons that will appear every time you start your computer.

A My Computer: Double-click here to see the contents of your computer (its disk drives, file folders, and removable storage—CDs and floppy disk drives). We'll examine all these later.

B My Documents: Double-click here to see the list of files you create, such as letters, reports, and pictures.

C Recycle Bin: Double-click here to see any file you've recently deleted—they're stored here for a while before Windows removes them completely. Nice to know in case you accidentally delete a file!

D Internet Explorer: Double-click here when you want to get online (something we'll look at in Chapter 3).

E My Network Places: Is your computer **networked** (connected to other computers)? If so, double-click here to see the other computers on the network.

F Start button: The nerve center of Windows. Single-click here to open the Start menu (see inset).

G Task bar: This bar displays buttons for every program you have open in Windows (such as the word processor you'll be using in Chapter 2)—but there aren't any running here.

H Status area: ("tray" to techies). Displays the system clock and little icons of special programs that are running. Click on these icons to run the programs, such as the computer's volume control, which is right next to the time here.

I **User name and icon:** The top of the Start menu identifies the user who has logged on, and it's one of the few icons in Windows that does nothing when you click it.

J **Programs:** All down the left side is a list of various programs. Click on any of these icons to launch a program. At the top is the permanent program list, here the Internet and e-mail software. In the middle is a list that changes to include only the six programs you have used most recently. And at the bottom is a little green triangle that you click to list all the programs on your computer. Brace yourself! It will be a lot.

K **File folders:** Here's another way to find those files you work with, including your pictures and music.

L **Functions:** The bottom right of the Start menu contains various Windows functions including the Control Panel and the ever-useful Help.

Windows explained

A double-glazed introduction to how your computer works

Microsoft Windows is the name of your computer's operating system—the software that tells your computer what to do. Think of it as the brains of the operation and a hyperactive butler all rolled into one. It's in charge of the computer, but it's there to do your bidding too. There are many versions of Windows (such as Windows 98 or Windows ME), but the one we'll be looking at is the most recent, Windows XP.

Why did Microsoft (the company that makes Windows software) name it after a sheet of glass? Good question! Well, it's because when you start opening programs on your computer, each box that springs up opens like, well, a window. Try it. Take your mouse and double-click on My Computer (look for the picture of a little computer). Voilà—you'll see a rectangular box open up containing a whole lot of other little icons.

At the top of the box is a strip of color with the words My Computer on it. This strip is called the **title bar**. Now look way over to the right of the title bar and you'll see three little squares—a line, a box, and an X. Click on the line. Whoa, where did the window go? Well, it's been **minimized**, meaning it's still running, but it's hidden. To get it back, move your mouse down to the bottom of your computer to the **task bar** and look for My Computer written out. Click on it and voilà, it's back. Now click on the middle square, and the whole screen fills up. That's what you call a **maximized** window. There are now two overlapping boxes next to the X. Click on that button and the window returns to normal size. If you click on the little X button, you'll close the window altogether. Here's a fun trick: Move the mouse over to the My Computer icon, hold down the left button, and drag the mouse way over to the right. The My Computer icon will move with the mouse. Now let go, and presto! It's there. Congratulations! You've mastered the click and drag.

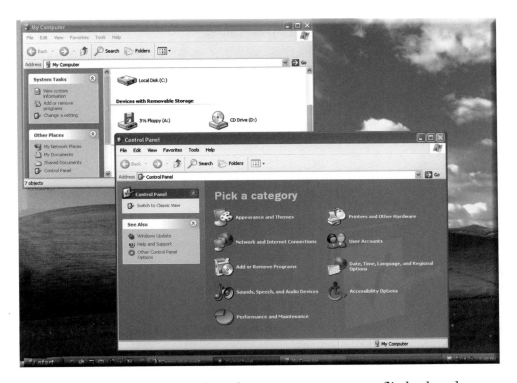

You can open up several windows at once, so you can flip back and forth between files. Here's how: Leave the My Computer window open and move the mouse over to Control Panel in the list at the left. Now click on it, and its window will open too. They may overlap a bit, but isn't that what real papers do on a desk?

loading software

A little software goes a long, long way

To cook, you need ingredients, bowls, an oven— the hardware of cooking so to speak. To create something edible you need a recipe. Think of software as your recipe. It tells your computer how to put things together the right way. Software can be divided into two main categories: an **operating system** to tell hardware how to function and **application program software** to show hardware how to perform specific tasks, like writing a letter.

The most popular operating system for computers is one you've probably heard of—Windows, as in Bill Gates, billionaire, Microsoft cofounder . . . You get the picture. Windows tells your computer how to operate. Chances are your computer already came with the Windows operating system **loaded** (a techie word that means installed).

Some of the hardware that you buy to work with your computer, such as the printer, also requires operating software to function. This software will come with your printer and will be in the form of either a **CD-ROM** or a **disk**—both "hold" or store the software. In order to make your printer work, you will have to insert the CD or diskette in the proper slot in your computer console or tower and then follow the install questions that will pop up on your screen. Easy as pie.

Even really good chefs rely on recipes to turn raw ingredients into a usable feast. That's just what software does. It puts all the ingredients together.

STEP BY STEP: LOADING SOFTWARE

1. Before installing new software, it's a good idea to shut down any programs that are running.

2. Open the software package—usually a shrink-wrapped box. Find the CD-ROM or disk inside.

3. Push the CD-ROM drive button on your console or tower so the CD-ROM tray comes out.

4. Place the CD-ROM in the tray's circle with the CD's writing side up. Gently push the tray back in.

Load your CD-ROM with its written side facing up. The opening slot directly under the CD-ROM tray is for floppy disks, which aren't floppy anymore, but the name stuck. Whatever you do, don't use the tray for a coffee cup holder.

5. Your computer will now make some noises, and after a while a new **window** or picture will pop up.

6. You will see some colorful graphics, usually with the name of the software on it. Click on where it says install. You will probably be asked to provide a registration number. That number can usually be found on the CD-ROM plastic case holder or in the instruction booklet. (Without a registration number the software won't install. This cuts down on software piracy.) Once your software is installed, it will remain on your hard drive until you delete it.

7. To access new software, you sometimes have to restart your computer. (Your software will tell you if you need to restart.) Go to the Start button and click on it (see page 32). A menu will pop up. Choose Restart. This will automatically restart your computer with your new software officially loaded.

8. To eject your CD-ROM disk, press the button on the CD-ROM drive. That will immediately eject it. If it gets stuck, look for a tiny little hole by the opening of the drive and insert the end of a paper clip into it to dislodge the CD-ROM disk.

THE THREE DRIVES

Inside the computer is something called the hard drive. It stores all your computer's operating software and your work. (It's also known as the C: drive.) So how does other software, such as word processing software, get in there? Through "external" drives, such as a floppy disk drive or CD-ROM drive for inserting software programs, as shown above. Software, whether from disks or CDs, is inserted into the computer via its respective drive and then "copied," or installed, onto your hard drive.

playing games

A game of Solitaire or Hearts is just a click away

What's the fastest and most enjoyable way to improve your new skills of clicking and dragging the mouse? Play a computer game. Windows XP contains four card games, a simulated pinball table, and an explosive game of chance called Minesweeper. Give them a whirl.

Ready to play?

- Click on the Start button.
- In the Start menu, click on All Programs.
- Find the menu there called Games. Click on it and look at the list. Whichever one you click on will launch a computer game.

You'll see five games with the word Internet in front (Internet Hearts, Checkers, Reversi and so on). These are multiplayer games you play against other people across the Internet. But for now, we'll stick with the solo games, and the most famous of these is Solitaire.

In Classic Solitaire, you have a deck and piles of cards with the top ones faceup. The aim of the game: Arrange the cards in descending order with black cards alternating with red cards. You

Computer Solitaire follows the same rules as the card game. Instead of shuffling and laying down cards, use your mouse and click and drag a card to its proper place. If you can't move, click on "Game" at the top, choose "Deal," and you'll be dealt new cards.

drag cards into place with your mouse from any of the piles. If you release a card too early (or try to cheat!), Windows will whiz the card back where it came from. Aces are placed in squares at the top right. Then, following suit, place twos on the aces, then threes, etc. Windows has another game called Spider Solitaire, which is more complex.

In Windows 3D Pinball you use the keyboard instead of buttons to work the ball. The Z and the forward slash (/) keys operate the left and right flippers. To launch the ball, you hold down the space bar, then release it. Other than that, the program's exactly like the arcade game.

Hearts mimics the four-player card game of the same name. When you first play this game, a dialogue box pops up with the message "Welcome to the Microsoft Hearts Network. What is your name?" Type your name in the white message box and click on OK. Now you'll see four hands, each labeled with a name. The object of the game is to get rid of all hearts cards and the Queen of Spades. Click on Help to explain the rest of the rules.

Minesweeper is a different game altogether. It's a bit like solo Battleship, only you're the one who stands to get blown up. Once you've got it open, click on any one square in the grid. If you're lucky, you'll get a "sweep," where lots of squares are cleared. Most people will just see a number in the square. This tells you how many bombs are next to the square—including diagonally. Click another square and try to figure out which squares have bombs under them. If you're unlucky, you'll be blown up instantly—each "minefield" has several bombs in it. You can mark any suspect square by right-clicking on it. A flag marker appears. When you've marked all the bombs and clicked off all the other squares, you've won!

FreeCell is a tricky sorting game, a bit like Solitaire. When it opens, you see eight columns of cards with eight empty "cells," or card-shaped holes. The idea is to sort all the cards into suit order in the four right-hand cells, using the others—the free cells—for holding one card apiece as you sort them. The trick is that the suits must all be in number order, starting with the ace. And as you're sorting the columns, you have to keep descending order there and alternate cards black-red-black. It's just as tricky as it sounds!

In the game Minesweeper, if you click on the wrong tile . . . kaboom! So use the numbers on the tiles to guide you. They tell you the number of mines that border their square.

plugging in your printer

It's easier than you think

Your printer is a pretty basic piece of equipment, so don't panic.
It's fairly easy to plug in and set up. First, find the printer cable. This is a thick cable with different-shaped connectors at either end. One connector end has 25 holes in it, and it plugs into the back of your computer. The other connector end plugs into the printer (usually its side or back). Note: Some new printers use USB connectors (see page 10). You plug the flat USB end into the computer and the square one into the printer.

- Turn on your printer first, then turn on your computer.

- When you turn on your computer, it should automatically recognize that there's a new printer plugged in. This instant recognition is something techies call **plug and play**.

- Now you are connected. Windows will now prompt you to install your printer software, which we explain on page 30.

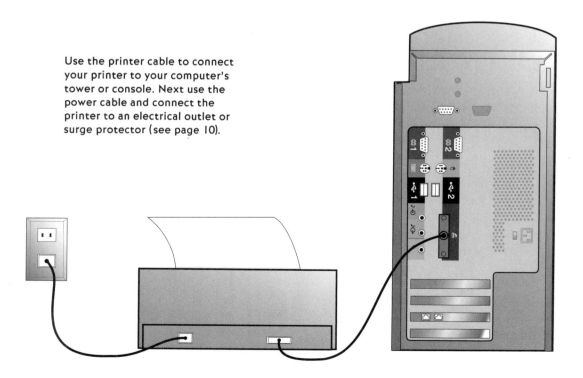

Use the printer cable to connect your printer to your computer's tower or console. Next use the power cable and connect the printer to an electrical outlet or surge protector (see page 10).

ASK THE EXPERTS

How do I care for my printer?

Printers are hungry creatures—they need to be fed two things: paper and ink. And you'll need to toss your printer a steady diet of these if you expect it to keep spitting out your carefully crafted pages. How you put the paper and ink (the so-called "consumables") into the printer varies depending on the model of printer you own—so you have to read the printer manual to do it properly.

There are many different types and models of printers. Some have you put the paper in a paper tray; others (like the one shown here) ask you to stack it on top of the printer in a paper feed.

How do I the load the paper?

The main paper source for your printer is the paper tray. Your **paper tray** may have a 50-sheet capacity or 100—whatever it is, stick to it. Overstuffing your paper tray will lead to a paper jam—which usually won't damage your printer, but will spoil your day.

How do I put in the ink?

Well, it depends on the kind of printer you have. **Laser printers** don't use ink at all—they print with a sooty powder called **toner** that's fused onto the paper, just as in a photocopier. The toner comes factory-inserted into a foot-long block of plastic called a **toner cartridge**. Inkjet printers drink their ink from plastic blocks the size of a package of cigarettes. Some inkjet printers have up to four inkjet cartridges—one each for black, red, blue, and yellow ink. When they are empty, you simply replace them.

setting up your printer

Congratulations! You've connected it all up. Now what? Not much, really! If you plugged your printer into your computer's USB port (the one with the skinny rectangular plug), Windows XP will find it as soon as you switch on both machines. When it does, it will automatically pop up a new window called Found New Hardware Wizard. (**Wizard** is the name for any program that takes you step-by-step through any process in Windows.) The New Hardware Wizard finds and installs the software your computer needs to run your printer—but you do have to help it along a little.

In each screen, and there will be a few, the Wizard gives you a couple of options, and one of them is usually labeled Recommended. Go with the recommendations unless your printer manual specifically tells you otherwise. See the little Next button at the bottom of the Wizard's window? Click it to move to the next step.

In broad steps, the Add New Hardware Wizard will want to find some special software, install it, and print out a test page to check that it's installed properly. The special software for a printer is called a **driver**—it's the set of codes that instruct the printer exactly how to print. Windows will take care of installing them, but you will have to slip a CD-ROM from the printer maker into your CD-ROM drive at the right time. When's the right time? Just before you click on the Next button on the Wizard screen that says it wants to look for printer software. Really . . . it's no trouble at all.

What if Windows doesn't automatically detect that you've added the printer? Don't panic. This will often happen if your printer has a parallel port plug—it's a bit chunky. In this case, you need to do a little more work:

1. Click on the Start button

2. Choose Control Panel (in the middle, on the right).

3. Click on Printers and Other Hardware

4. Under Pick a Task, select Add a Printer.

5. The Add Printer Wizard will appear. Click the Next button.

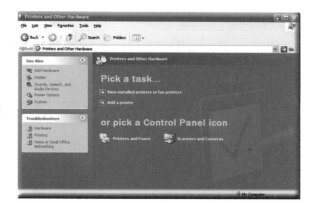

6. Stick with the options that are already checked (Local printer, automatically detect and install) unless your printer maker instructs you any differently. Click the Next button.

7. The Wizard will detect the printer and offer to install it. Make sure the CD-ROM containing your printer software is inserted. Then click on Next.

The Wizard will take care of everything from here on out. Just wait for the final step (the one with a button labeled Finish), and you'll be set. Congratulations! You're now ready to print.

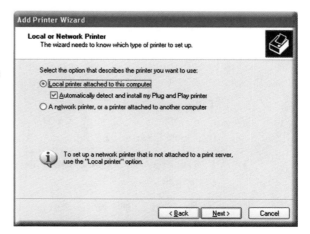

turning it off

To stop you gotta go to Start

Sure, you can hit the Off button, but it's not recommended.
That would be like yanking out the ignition keys of your car while it's still in drive. When you want to turn off your car, you need to put it in Park first. Same with the computer—you need to put it in Park before you can turn it off. That means going down to the **task bar** at the bottom of the screen. Click on the Start button. Yes, it's a bit counterintuitive, but you have to use the Start button to turn off the computer. Follow the steps below and then push the Off buttons on the monitor and console or tower.

Start menu

Start button

Turn Off command

Task bar

1. Click once on the Start button. The Start menu will pop up. Click on Turn Off Computer (it's down in the bottom right corner).

2. A little window appears, labeled Turn Off Computer.

3. Click once on the red Turn Off button. Sometimes a little window called a dialogue box will appear asking you if you're sure you want to. Click OK or Yes.

4. Most newer computers will then turn themselves off automatically. Some will show a black screen stating "It is now safe to turn off your computer." If you see the message, press the Off button on your tower or console.

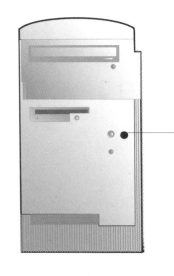

Push the On/Off button on the tower and the computer shuts down. (Some do this automatically when you click on Shut down.)

Shut off the monitor by pushing the On/Off button.

HAT IF

You decide you don't want to shut the computer down when you see the Shut Down box?

Press the Esc key on the upper left corner of the keyboard to return to the desktop. Or click the Cancel button on the menu.

You turn the computer off with the power button instead of using the Start menu to shut the computer down?

It's not a catastrophe, but doing it can damage your files (more on them in Chapter 2). Try to avoid doing it.

You want to restart the computer instead of shut down?

Click once on the Restart command and then click the OK button. It will shut down and start back up automatically—taking you to the log-on box.

You came back after answering your door and your computer screen is black. Did it shut itself off?

No, it's **sleeping,** an energy-saving mode that spares your monitor and computer. To wake up your computer, touch any key or move the mouse, and it will come to life.

now what do I do?

Answers to common problems

I spilled coffee on my keyboard. What can I do?

You should turn the computer off and disconnect the keyboard. Turn the keyboard over and try to wipe off as much liquid as you can—you might try using Q-Tips, tissues, or even a blow-dryer. Then plug the keyboard back in and turn the computer on. If some keys don't work, you will probably need to buy a new keyboard (starts around $20), because it will most likely cost that much or more to get the keyboard fixed.

My computer just stopped working and the screen froze. What can I do?

Don't panic. This happens. Computer techies call this **crashing**. Most of the time, Windows XP is just wondering what to do next, so don't panic; just wait one minute until the screen unfreezes again and all your software programs are up and running. If just one program stays frozen, you can stop that program and restart it. To stop a program, hold down the Ctrl, Alt, and Delete keys at the same time. The Windows Task Manager will pop up, showing a list of applications (another word for programs)

that are running. Click on the offending item and click the End Task button. Presto! The program will vanish, and you can restart.

My mouse keeps sticking on the mouse pad. What can I do?

Turn the mouse over and look for the arrows on the circular piece of plastic. There should be a hole in the plastic (this is where the roller ball touches the mouse pad). Turn the piece of plastic in the direction of the arrows, and the mouse will open up. Take the roller ball out and wipe it off with a clean cloth; scrape any grime off the rollers with a pencil eraser. Replace the roller ball and plastic piece, and the mouse should roll better now. If this doesn't work, you might just need to buy another mouse (usually under $20).

Do I have to turn the computer off every time I finish working?

You don't have to turn the computer off every day. It is actually better on the computer circuits to leave it running instead of turning it off and on all the time. Just keep in mind that you should shut down the computer regularly (once a week) so that the hard disk and memory can get "cleaned" up.

How do I set the date and time on my computer?

You know where the clock is? It's down there in the corner at the end of the task bar. Double-click on it (click twice in rapid succession). The Date and Time Properties window will appear, giving you the chance to change the day, month, year on one side, and the clock on the other. To change the time, double-click on one group of the numbers (hour, minute, or second). A blue selection box will appear over the number. Just type in the correct time and it will overwrite the old one. Better still, if your computer's hooked up to the Internet, click on the Internet Time tab at the top of the screen, and click on the Update Now button to synchronize your computer's clock with an atomic clock on the Internet. Very cool.

HELPFUL RESOURCES

CONTACTS	BOOKS
Microsoft support Windows XP (425) 635-3311 Windows 98 (425) 635-7222	**PCs for Dummies** By Dan Gookin **Teach Yourself Computer Basics** By Jill T. Freeze

Writing a letter

2

The computer's blank screen is somehow less
daunting than a real piece of blank paper.
Maybe that's because it's so easy to fix your mistakes
on a computer. You can even change the tabs,
check for spelling errors, and select new fonts.
All these things and more you'll discover
in this chapter.

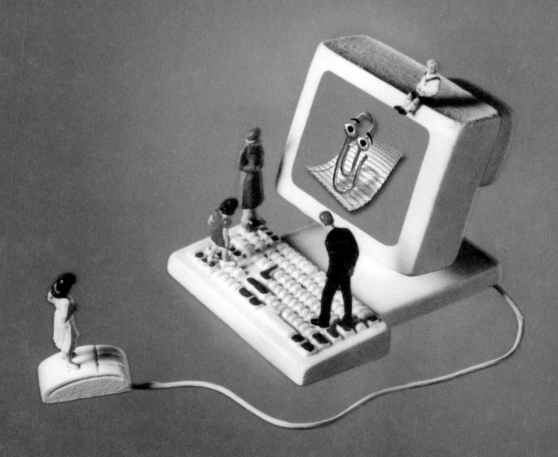

the blank page

*Word processing . . .
it beats the fastest
typewriter every time*

Here's how to get to a blank document so you can start writing. Depending on the word processing software you have, you will most likely begin by clicking the Start button—the button at the lower left of your desktop page. Next, move the cursor to All Programs, and click on the arrow. Then move the cursor over again onto the word processing software program you have in your hard drive—for example, Microsoft Word, Microsoft Works, Corel WordPerfect, or Lotus WordPro. When you see your word processing program, click on it.

Once the program has been selected and clicked, it will automatically open (computerspeak for begin). You'll see a snazzy graphic with the software's name on it and then . . . ta-da, a blank screen with a tiny vertical bar flashing on it. Called a **cursor**, this bar follows your typing. Think of it as signpost, always letting you know where you are. There will also be an I-beam that represents the mouse pointer. To complicate things (as if they aren't complicated enough), the mouse pointer is also called a cursor! Don't worry. We'll help you through it all.

Like your fifth grade teacher's pointer, the computer's cursor "points" to where you are typing on the page.

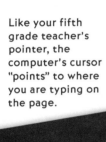

# ASK THE EXPERTS

My computer didn't come with word processing software. Can I still write a letter?

Yes, you can. There is a generic word processing program that comes with Windows XP, called WordPad. To find it, click the Start button, move your cursor over so it highlights All Programs, and click the arrow. Then move the cursor over so it highlights Accessories. Then click on WordPad. It should open right up and present you with a blank page. Start writing that letter!

I bought the latest word processing software. How do I install it?

Most computers come with word processing software. If yours doesn't, you'll have to install it yourself. Relax, breathe. It's easy. Software these days comes on CD-ROMs, or hard round disks that look just like music CDs. To insert or **load** the software, find your CD-ROM drive on your computer console or tower. Push the button, and a tray automatically springs out; place the CD-ROM disk in the tray and close it. Your CD-ROM will start making noises, and then suddenly a picture of the software will appear on your screen. Simply follow the installation instructions. This involves clicking a few "Yes" or "OK" or "Next" boxes after each computer **prompt** (or question). (See pages 24–25 for more detail.)

How do I stop my word processor?

Look at the top right-hand corner of your document and you'll see three boxes. The first contains a small dash, the second a square, and the third an X. Click on the last box and you will immediately be asked if you want to save the changes you've made. Click No, and you're outta there.

PRINT IT

If you want to see what you've just typed on paper, simply use your mouse and go up to the File command in the upper left-hand corner. Click on File, scroll down until you find Print, and click. You'll see a box with information in it. It will tell you the name of your printer in the top bar. Click on OK, and in just a few seconds, you'll see your work at hand. You are now computer literate! (See page 52 for more detailed instructions).

the filled page

Hit the keys and start the Great American Novel

So now you're all set to type! Great! Try a letter to a friend extolling your newfound computer skills. Notice that when you have typed enough words to fill a line, it automatically spills it over to the next line. This is called **wrapping the text** and is one of the many conveniences of a word processor versus a typewriter. You don't have to hit a carriage return at the end of each line.

If you want to force-start a new line, as for a new paragraph, press the large Enter key on your keyboard. Or you can press the Enter key twice, and there'll be a blank line before you start typing the next paragraph (as in the picture below). After you've typed a few lines, your friendly **Office Assistant** (a built-in feature in some word processing software) will pop up to help you style your letter.

If you want to move the cursor within the text, use the **arrow** keys on the keyboard. These are the keys with the four arrows, located to the right of the space bar. They can move the cursor in any direction—up, down, right, left. You can also move directly to a new place in the text by clicking the mouse—you place the mouse pointer right where you want the cursor to be and click once.

Here's a typical letter. Notice how it all lines up on the left side of the page. Notice, too, that green wavy line under "that." Your word processing software is alerting you to a potential grammatical or spelling error.

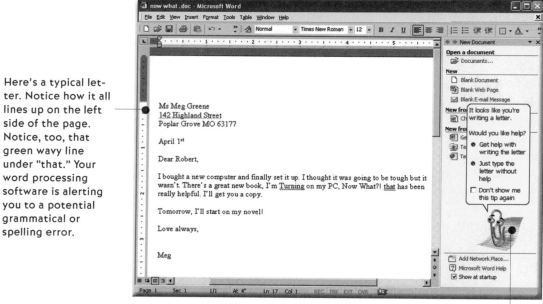

The goofy looking paper clip guy that pops up after a few lines is called the Office Assistant.

ASK THE EXPERTS

Who is the paper clip dude?

If you have started the Microsoft Word word processor for the first time, the Office Assistant (cute little guy that looks like a paper clip) should automatically pop up on-screen and ask you what you would like to do. The Office Assistant is a quick way to search for help on a particular topic and find shortcuts.

If you don't see the Office Assistant, simply click the Microsoft Word Help button [?] on the tool bar. If the Microsoft Word Help window pops up instead (which is another way to get help with this program), that just means that you need to activate the Office Assistant manually. Close the Help window by clicking the Close button [x].

Click onto Help on the menu bar at the top of the screen and select the Show the Office Assistant command. He will stay on your desktop as long as you want him to—or as long as you need his help, that is. Simply type your question into the white box on his voice bubble and click the Search button. Click on one of the options he gives you, and this should answer your question.

How do I get rid of Mr. Paper Clip?

To hide him, right-click on your mouse above his icon. When the menu appears, select the Hide Assistant option. To make him come back, click on the Help button.

saving your work

The mysterious world of files and folders explained

When you save a word processing document, such as a letter to Mom, it gets converted into something called a **file**— computerspeak for a saved document. So whenever you want to save your work, go up to the **menu** bar (the bar of words at the top of your computer) and click on File. Move down until you see Save and click on it. A **save** box will appear with the first few words of your document highlighted in the bottom of the box, next to "file name." You'll probably want to name it something else. Just type over the name of the file and then click the Save button on the top right of the box. Your precious document is now saved.

Your next task is to decide where to store this thrilling new file. Otherwise, how will you find it again? Well, just as in real life where paper files are usually stored in **folders**, so it is with computers: ergo, computer files are stored in computer folders. In fact, Windows, your friendly operating software, will usually select the My Documents folder to store your files in. The minute you click the Save button, a copy of your file is stored in your My Documents folder. We'll tell you how to find it again on page 46.

You have to click in the Save file to get the Save dialogue box in order to save your work.

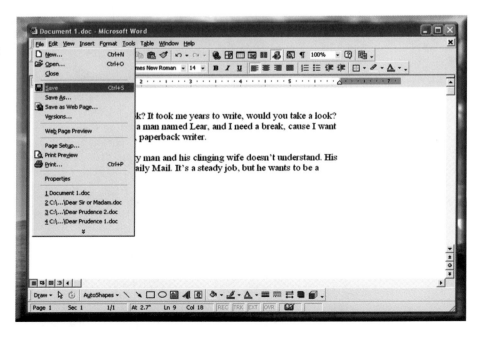

WHAT IF

Everything on the page moved over and you can't read it. What happened?

You probably accidentally hit the scroll bar. A simple fix: Go to the menu bar and click on Edit and scroll down till you see Undo Typing. Click on that. You should be back to normal.

You don't want to save your document to the My Documents folder. Where else can you save it?

Go up to File on the menu bar and click on Save As. A list will pop down. On this list you will see Desktop. If you want to save it to your desktop, click on that.

You want to rename your file. How do you do this?

Go to File, and instead of clicking on Save, click on Save As. Then type in the new name you want, click on the Save button, and it will automatically rename the document. It will also keep a copy of the document under its old name.

FIRST PERSON DISASTER

Save As You Go

I was finally getting around to writing up what I had been doing for the last fifteen years for my college's class notes. Doing it on the computer was wonderful because you can edit your writing so easily. No more retyping things over and over again. I was just about done when it started to thunder. The rain was coming down in torrents. I saw the lights flicker and went to check on the house. All was well, but when I got back to my computer the screen was blank—as if I hadn't spent all morning typing up my life. What happened? A call to my son confirmed the worst. My college letter was lost because I hadn't stopped periodically while typing it to save it. He said when the lights flickered, my computer probably experienced a power surge and temporarily shut down. When that happens any work that isn't saved is lost. He suggested hitting the save button every five to ten minutes or so.

Pat L., New Smyrna Beach, Florida

editing your work

Changing your mind has never been so easy

No more ripping the paper out of the typewriter and starting all over. Just a click here and a few there and presto, it's now just what you wanted. For example, to delete letters or words, place the cursor at the end of the text you want to remove, and then press the Backspace key until it is gone. Or place the cursor at the beginning of the text you want to remove and press the Delete key. Basically, the **Backspace** key deletes characters to the left of the insertion point, and the **Delete** key deletes characters to the right of the insertion point. Or you can use your mouse to find the text you want to delete. Hold the left button down and drag it across all the words you want erased. This will highlight the letters or words (show them in reverse, white letters on black). Then press the Delete key.

I Say you want to delete this address. First you highlight it (start at Dr. and drag your mouse across the entire address).

2 Now press the Delete key on the keyboard. And poof, it's gone. If you want it back, you will have to retype it.

3 To move the address so it's under the date, highlight it. Then click on Cut (the scissors icon).

4 Next, move your cursor to where you want the address to be and click on that spot. Now click on Paste (the clipboard icon).

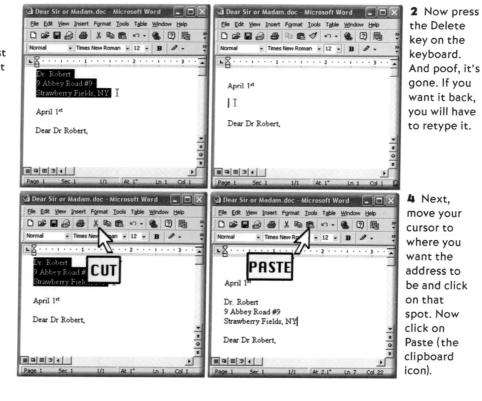

Perhaps you want to insert new text in the middle of a passage. This is done easily by placing the cursor's insertion point in the text where you want to add information, then click—and just begin typing. It is that simple. You will see that any text that follows what you are adding will simply move to the right. Here's another nice tip. If you hate the sentence you just wrote, you can type in a new one without first deleting the old one. Just touch the **Insert** key, the one to the right of the backspace key. Type your new words over the old ones. When you're done, be sure to press Insert again, or you will keep erasing the words on the screen.

You can also **move** words, sentences, paragraphs, even whole pages around if you want. To do this, use your mouse to click on the beginning part of text you want to move. Drag the mouse until the entire word or all the words you want to move are highlighted. While the text remains highlighted, move your cursor to the scissors icon on the tool bar (see Fig. 3 on opposite page). Click on it, and the text will instantly disappear. Don't panic. It will come back. Move your mouse back to your text and put the cursor where you want the mysteriously removed text to go, then click. Now go back up to the tool bar and click on the clipboard icon. Voilà! Your missing text will magically reappear.

ASK THE EXPERTS

What is the Copy button?

The Copy button next to the scissors—it looks like two pieces of paper—works much like the Cut button. You highlight the text you want to copy. Then click Copy. Move your cursor back to the text where you want the words repeated and click. Then go up to Paste and click. You can paste over and over again. Gives new meaning to having to write "I will not talk in class" 50 times on the blackboard.

What if I make some terrible mistake, such as accidentally deleting a big chunk of text?

There's a neat button called Undo in the middle of the row of buttons at the top of your screen. It looks like an arrow curving to the left. Hit that, and whatever you did last is undone. That chunk of text will pop right back.

finding files

No more unclaimed treasures, no more searches through lost-and-found

Opening and closing documents is like opening your desk drawer. You open a drawer, locate the file, read it and make any changes to it, then put it back in the folder and close the drawer. Your computer operates the same way. It stores all your files and keeps them in the same location, ready for use.

Each time you want to work with a document, you need to open it. To do this, click the File menu and select the **Open** command. This will display an Open dialogue box, where you can choose from the files in your My Documents folder.

There are two easy ways to open the file you want: Either click once on the file name and then click the Open button, or double-click on the file. When the document opens, you can make any changes to it you want. When you finish working on it, click on the **Save** icon that looks like a floppy disk, then close it by clicking on File, then on Close. If you forgot to hit the Save icon, don't worry. The computer will ask if you want to save your changes. Click the Yes button, and your file is saved. Of course, if you've changed your mind and don't want to save any of the changes you've just slaved over, click on No, and those once-brilliant changes will disappear and you'll be back to your old file.

Filing papers in real life can be a real challenge for some; thankfully, it's a whole lot easier with a computer.

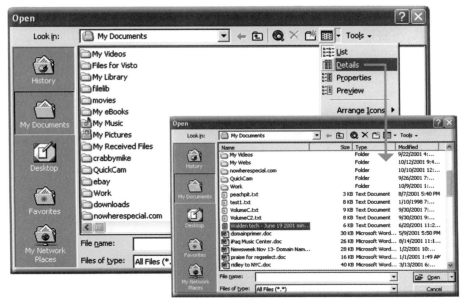

Don't like the way your programs list files in the File Open dialogue box? Click on the View icon and pick another option. The Details view shows you the most—including the size and type of file you're looking at, and when it was last worked on.

 **HAT IF**

You want to open more than one file (within the same folder) at a time?

You can do this. Just hold down the Ctrl key while you click on each file you want to open, then click the Open button. All the files will open up in your word processor like a flower.

You opened two files but can't see the one you want?

To show the file you want to work on, click the Window button and find the name in the drop-down list. Click on it.

You want to open a file you recently worked on?

Click on the File menu. You will see a list of the five most recently opened files. Click on the one you want, and it will come up on your screen.

creating a letter

Your word processing software will automatically set the margins, choose the type, and flush left all the text of every letter or document you write. If you'd like to change these **default** (automatic) settings, here's how:

CHANGING FONTS AND SIZES:

Changing fonts: Highlight the text whose font you want to change, by clicking and dragging the mouse across the selected text. Then use your mouse and go up to the Menu bar, where you will find the name of the highlighted font in a box. Click and hold on the arrow to the right of the font box, and a list will drop down. Drag down to one of the font choices and release the mouse. All the type that is highlighted in your letter will change to that font.

Changing font size: Highlight the type. Go up to the Menu bar. The number in the box to the right of the font box shows the size of the highlighted font. Click and hold on the arrow to the right of the font size box and a menu of font sizes will appear. Drag down to one of the font sizes and release the mouse. All the type that is highlighted will change to that size.

SPACING: Your letter will be automatically single-spaced. To create more space between the lines, called double-spacing, highlight all the words in your letter. Go up to the Menu bar and click and hold on Format. Go down to Paragraph and release the mouse. A dialogue box will appear. Go to line spacing. Click on the arrow, slide down to "double," and let go. The lines in your letter will now be spaced farther apart.

THE ASSISTANT: An animated helper who can offer advice and answer questions when you're in trouble.

A MARGINS: To set the left margin, go up to the ruler and click on the little square at the far left and drag it where you want it. To set the right, drag the little triangle at the far right.

B ALIGNMENT: To center your name and address at the top of the page, click and hold to highlight all the lines. Let go of the mouse. Go up the the menu bar and click on the button that shows the lines of type centered.

Your address will move to the center of the page.

C INDENTING: For a simple way to indent the first line of a paragraph, place the cursor in front of the paragraph and push the Tab key once. Do this with each of the paragraphs in your letter.

D MAKING BOLD: To emphasize a word or words to make them stand out, click and drag to highlight the words and let go. Go up the the Menu bar and click on the capital B.

B _I_ U

The words you selected will appear heavier—this is called boldface. If you want to make a word stand out by having it in slanted letters, click on the capital I (for italics). To underline the word, click on the underlined U.

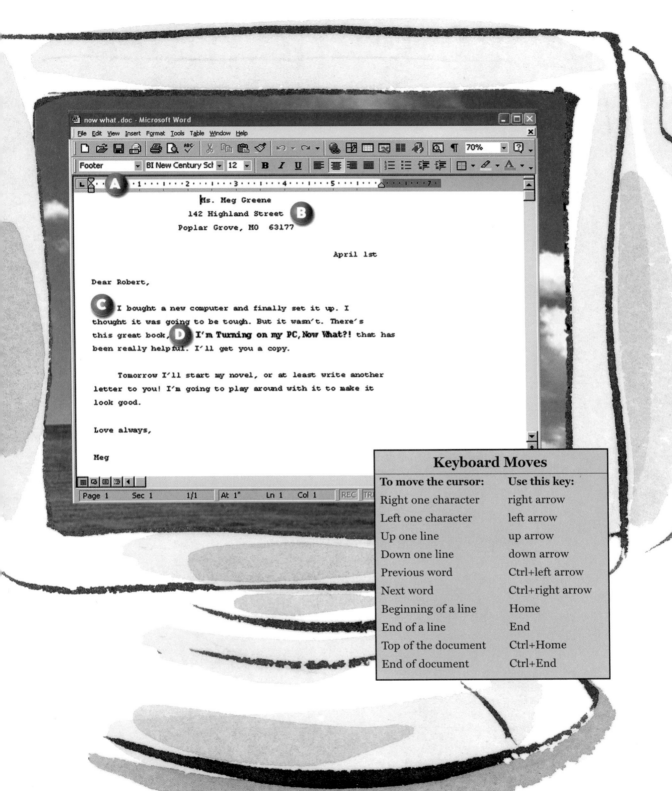

now what .doc - Microsoft Word

File Edit View Insert Format Tools Table Window Help

Footer   BI New Century Sch   12   **B** *I* <u>U</u>

Ms. Meg Greene
142 Highland Street
Poplar Grove, MO 63177

April 1st

Dear Robert,

I bought a new computer and finally set it up. I thought it was going to be tough. But it wasn't. There's this great book, **I'm Turning on my PC, Now What?!** that has been really helpful. I'll get you a copy.

Tomorrow I'll start my novel, or at least write another letter to you! I'm going to play around with it to make it look good.

Love always,

Meg

Page 1   Sec 1   1/1   At 1"   Ln 1   Col 1   REC

Keyboard Moves

To move the cursor:	Use this key:
Right one character	right arrow
Left one character	left arrow
Up one line	up arrow
Down one line	down arrow
Previous word	Ctrl+left arrow
Next word	Ctrl+right arrow
Beginning of a line	Home
End of a line	End
Top of the document	Ctrl+Home
End of document	Ctrl+End

spelling and more

Just because you speak English doesn't mean you write it real good

Have you ever written something and then gone back and read it later, only to find numerous spelling blunders, obvious typos, and painfully blatant punctuation errors? Ouch. Nearly everyone makes typing mistakes when using a word processor. The good news is that these mistakes are so easy to fix. No more ripping up and starting over.

Most word processors come with **language tools** (fancy talk for programs that, among other things, check the spelling in your document, count the number of words in it, or point out any grammatical problems). To spell check your letter, go up to the Menu bar and click on Tools. Move your cursor down until you see **Spelling and Grammar** and click on it. This feature will scan your letter for misspelled words or strange grammatical constructions. When it finds something wrong, it will highlight the word or phrase and tell you the problem, for example, a repeated word or a word not in the dictionary. (Beware—the spell checker will flag slang words not in the dictionary.) It will then offer suggested fixes. You can click on either Ignore if you think you are right or Change if you agree with the computer.

The **Thesaurus** is a convenient tool that helps you replace a word with a more suitable one. To use it, move your mouse over the word in question and click on it so it becomes highlighted. Then move the mouse up to the Menu bar and click on Tools. Scroll down to Language, then scroll again to Thesaurus. The computer will look up the highlighted word and find synonyms that might be more accurate.

Most word processing software provides spelling and grammar checks as well as a thesaurus to help improve the readability of your documents. Think of it as your personal in-house editor.

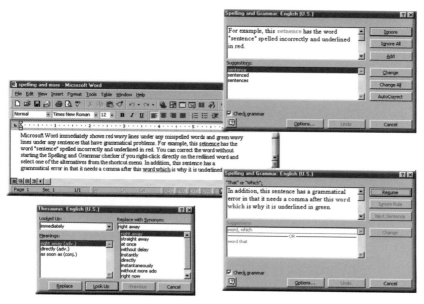

FLAGGIN' WORDS

Proper nouns are words that are specific names, such as a person's name (Barbara), a company's name (Barnes & Noble), or a product's name (Ford's Explorer). These types of words will usually trip up the spelling and grammar checker. They aren't found in the dictionary, so they will be flagged in your document. This doesn't mean that they are incorrect; it just means that your word processor's language tool isn't sophisticated enough to know whether or not a word is a proper noun.

When you click on spell check and grammar check, your computer will take you through your document. It will highlight any misspelled words or words it deems ungrammatical. You can either accept its changes or click the Ignore button.

ASK THE EXPERTS

Can my computer tell right away that a word is spelled incorrectly?

Many word processors immediately show wavy lines under any word or group of words that they think are misspelled or grammatically problematic. This way, you immediately see the problem while you are typing.

How can I tell how many words I've written?

Go to the Menu bar and under Tools scroll down till you find Word Count, and click. It will automatically count the number of words in the file. If you are interested in finding the number of words in a particular sentence or paragraph, simply highlight those words or sentences and go to Word Count. It will calculate only the number of highlighted words.

printing a letter

Seeing your words on paper

When you print your document, it's the real deal.
You can see it, touch it, and even crumple it up and throw it in the trash. Before you print your document, you should preview it. **Print Preview**, as word processors call it, is when the word processor displays on your monitor screen how the document will look.

Print Preview is a great way to review your work before you waste paper. Is that the font (or style of type) you wanted? Are the margins too wide? To preview your document, click the File menu and select Print Preview.

Word processors make it easy to print a document. You can print the whole document, a single page, or specific pages. You can also specify the number of copies to print, and you can collate the copies as you print. You'll see all of these options clearly described in the middle of the Print dialogue box.

To print your document, click the File menu and select Print—this will open the Print dialogue box, where you can select different printing options. Specify the document pages you want printed and click the OK button.

It takes about two hours to print out a copy of the New Testament—a task that would ordinarily have taken a medieval monk several years.

 # WHAT IF

You find a small typo while viewing your document in Print Preview?

Close the Print Preview window to go back to the document and make your fix. Save it and then print it.

You want to make a change to one page in a report after you've printed out the whole report?

You don't have to reprint the whole report. Go to the page in question and make your correction. With that page still on your screen, click on Print; now click the circle beside Current page to put a dot in it. That is the only page that will print.

You get an error message when you print?

If you try to print but get a message telling you that the program has tried to print and it won't work, click the Help button on that message screen. Follow the series of questions to find out what might be wrong with your printer. It could be that you didn't connect the printer correctly, that you didn't set the printer up correctly, or that the printer is simply out of paper.

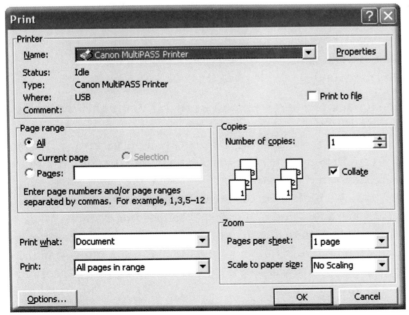

The Print dialogue box allows you to set different printing options for your document.

now what do I do?

Answers to common problems

How do I start and stop my word processing program?

Depending on the word processing program you have, you will most likely need to click Start, point to Programs, and click on Microsoft Word, Microsoft Works, Corel WordPerfect, or Lotus WordPro. If you don't have one of these word processing programs, click the Accessories subfolder and click on WordPad. The program will start automatically. To stop the program when you are finished, click the X button in the top right corner of the program window—just as you do when you want to close any window.

Do I have to start and stop the program each time I want to create a new document?

When you want to create a new document while you are already working in a document, click the mouse pointer on the word File on the Menu bar and select the New command. This will open a new document.

How can I save my Microsoft Word file so that my friend using a different program can read it?

You need to convert your file to the format that your friend is using, say, for example, Corel WordPerfect. Your word processor should come with many different converters, which are software utilities that help the different software programs talk to each other. Start by saving the document as a different file name. When you are in the Save box, click Save As. Go to the Type drop-down list at the bottom of the box and choose, for example, WordPerfect. It is that easy.

I want to replace the same name I used 10 times throughout my letter. How can I do it?

Many word processors come with a Search and Replace feature. For example, if you wrote a cover letter to one company and want to tailor the letter to send it to another company, you could save time by replacing the name of the company you are sending it to. Click on Edit from the Menu bar and select the Replace command. Type the text you want to find in the Find What box (for example, cake), then type the text you want to replace it with in the Replace With box (for example, pie). You can then click the Find Next button to find the next text example and then click Replace to replace them one at a time (or you can click the Replace All button to find and replace them all at once).

How can I copy a portion of one letter into a different letter?

Essentially, you want to cut and paste between different files. First open the file that has the text you want to copy. Highlight it. Now hold down the Ctrl key and press the C key. Your text has now been copied to the clipboard. What's a clipboard? It's an out-of-the-way place where Windows puts the last item you cut or copied. Now, to put the copied text into a new file, simply open the new file and put your cursor where you want the text to appear. Next hold down the Ctrl key and press the V key, and the copied material will be pasted in.

What are the different types of font?

A font is a complete collection of letters, punctuation marks, numbers, and special characters with a consistent and identifiable typeface distinguished by weight (such as **bold**), posture (such as *italic*), and size. There are three basic kinds of fonts: serif, sans serif, and script. Serif type has little edges that stick out from the ends of each letter; sans serif doesn't. Script type looks like handwriting.

Here are examples of each kind:

- Serif: Times New Roman   Courier
- Sans serif: Arial
- Script: *Brush Script Bold*

HELPFUL RESOURCES

CONTACTS	BOOKS
Microsoft **Desktop Applications** (425) 454-2030	**Windows XP** **for Dummies** By Woody Leonhard
Office for Windows (425) 635-7056	

Internet

3

In just a few pages the wonders of the Internet are yours for the taking. First there are a few decisions to be made, such as selecting an online service provider and choosing a Web browser. What are we talking about, you cry? Fret not. All will be explained. And then get ready for serious fun with surfing, shopping, and chatting online.

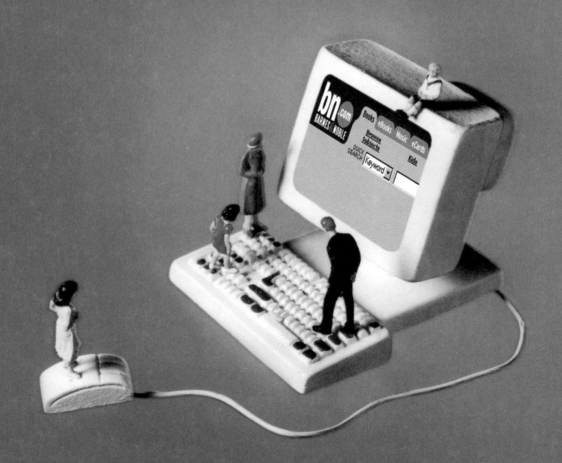

what is the Internet?

What is it, and why should I care?

If the Internet is the new information super-highway, then your computer is just one of the many cars rattling down it. It doesn't matter whether you are driving a Rolls or a Hyundai. All cars are welcome, and all drivers are treated equally.

So what exactly is the Internet? Well, it's best explained by its nickname, the Information Superhighway. It's like a huge highway that wraps around the entire world, with zillions of connecting byways, main streets, even dirt tracks. Instead of cars and trucks, little packets of computer information are going along the paths carrying pictures, programs, text, and sounds from anywhere in the world to your computer. Like a real road system, the Internet gets occasional traffic jams, but usually you can go another way.

How do you get onto this highway? You need an **Internet Service Provider** (sometimes called an ISP; more on those on pages 64–65), which provides an on-ramp for your computer to get onto the highway. Once you're online, you can use an electronic mail program to exchange messages and use a program called a **Web browser** to visit **Web pages**. These pages contain text and pictures. And Web pages also contain **links** to other Web pages. These links are often underlined in blue text; click on a link (more on these later) and you'll find yourself, ta-da, on another Web page. It's these links that gave rise to the Web's name—if you imagine all the links in all the pages as lines, you'd have a mass of threads as intricate as a spiderweb.

# ASK THE EXPERTS

How did the Internet come about?

Back in the 1960s two trends that seem unrelated gave birth to the Information Superhighway we know today. A few universities across the United States had just developed **supercomputers** (computers that can process huge amounts of data quickly), and the academic world wanted to share their research and computing power. So the supercomputer centers **networked,** or linked up, with each other and allowed other, less powerful, computers to access them. Meanwhile, the U.S. Department of Defense wanted to create a channel of communication that could withstand heavy bombing and still be able to carry military intelligence back and forth. So they developed a network too. When the two networks joined together, they became the Internet. Since then millions and millions of smaller networks have joined in, and things have never been the same.

Is the Internet the same thing as the Web?

No, it's not. The Internet is like a network of roads that carry information. The biggest use of the Internet continues to be delivering pieces of electronic mail (e-mail). The World Wide Web also uses the Internet roadway, but instead of simple mail messages, it lets you stop and explore (i.e., browse) the sights in graphic detail, for example, photos of things for sale at online stores, news videos, and audio clips.

Who invented the Internet?

It's hard to give the credit to one person or organization, because so many people were involved. The U.S. Department of Defense takes some credit—they put up the cash to create a network that would work even if bombs were dropped on a lot of communications lines. Vinton Cerf came up with the rules of the road (the Internet protocols) that let different computers exchange information, which earned him the honorary title of Father of the Internet. And a physicist called Tim Berners-Lee came up with the idea (and name) of the World Wide Web.

getting connected

To dial up Mom, use the phone; to dial up the world, use a modem

Imagine being able to send letters, photos, videos over the phone! What a world that would be. Well, ahem, it's here. But instead of using your phone, you use your personal computer. Almost every computer you can buy these days contains a piece of internal hardware called a **modem** that's designed to plug into your phone wall outlet, dial up your Internet service provider, and bring the Internet into your home.

All you need to get online is a bit of phone wire long enough to reach from the wall socket to the back of your computer. Plug one end into the wall socket and the other into the modem port. You'll see there are two ports (computerspeak for openings, or sockets). Make sure you don't use the one that's labeled with a stencil of a telephone (that's for a separate phone line if you want). Once your modem is tapped into Ma Bell, you are set to go online (connect up to the Internet). Whenever you are online, your phone line is in use, so you can't make or receive phone calls. Once you're done with the Internet, you can use the phone again.

When your modem is ready to roll, you're all set to hook up with a service provider. But first, you need to know how fast your modem runs. Most modems these days are rated at 56,000 bits per second (sometimes called 56K). Some older ones top out at 33,600 bits per second. When you come to select a dial-up number with your service provider, these numbers will be important. If you just got a new computer, just assume its modem runs at 56K. Before you make the final jump onto the Internet, consider two much faster ways to get online. One uses your TV cable line to transfer Internet information, and the other uses a souped-up phone line. Computer folks call these faster connections **broadband.** Think of them as wide multilane highways compared to the narrow "dirt track" of a 56K modem connection. In fact, these connections are quite a bit faster—cable Internet can top 1,500,000 bits per second, or 1550K. That's more than 25 times as fast as a regular 56K connection.

Ask THE EXPERTS

What should I do if I want to get calls while I'm online?

You'll have to have another phone line installed that you can reserve just for the Internet. Or you can connect up via your cable company or via a newer phone technology called DSL.

I've heard that my cable company gives Internet access. What gives?

It's true. Many cable companies can give you fast access to the Internet with a so-called broadband connection. This can be up to 25 times faster than dialing up using a modem, and it doesn't tie up your phone line. But there are some steps you need to know about.

1. You must plug your computer into a special cable modem, a boxy thing about the size of this book but twice as thick. The cable guy will bring this when he sets you up.

2. This cable modem must plug into a **network card** in your computer (also called an Ethernet card). If you don't have one, the cable guy may be able to fix you up.

3. Someone must program your computer's settings so it can communicate through the network card and cable modem to the service provider. Don't panic! The cable company will take care of this!

Network Card

going online

Learn about the new phone companies of the Internet

To use your telephone, you need the phone company to provide you with phone service. The same goes for your modem. But instead of Ma Bell connecting you, you need to sign up with a company that will provide Internet service—either an **Internet Service Provider** (or ISP) or an **online service** (America Online, Earthlink, CompuServe, and The Microsoft Network are some of the main ones).

What is Internet service? Well, it basically gives you access via your phone line to a big Internet computer that is linked to other Internet computers all over the world. Both an ISP and an online service will give you the telephone number of a computer near you that your modem can dial into to provide access to the Internet. (You want your computer to dial a local number so you won't have to pay long-distance charges each time you go online.) Some providers charge a flat monthly fee, while others charge by the hour. Part of this service includes an e-mail account. (See Chapter 4.)

Regardless of the type of service you choose, you will need to come up with two important things: your user name and password. A user name can be your last name or a made-up name. To protect your Internet privacy, we suggest you use a made-up user name, perhaps a nickname or your initials. Just make sure you won't mind giving it out as your e-mail address. Your password can be any word or set of numbers you can remember easily.

Think of your online service provider as your own personal operator who puts your calls through over the Internet.

SK THE EXPERTS

Can someone eavesdrop on me while I'm online?

The risk of someone tracing where you surf online or reading what you write in chat rooms is pretty remote. For it to happen, a secret program has to be hidden in a suspect Web site—the kind run by shady characters. This is one of the many reasons why you should not visit Web sites listed in e-mail messages from people you don't know.

If I get an Internet account, can someone get into my computer files without my knowing it?

Any unauthorized entry into someone else's computer files is called **hacking** and is a federal offense. Hackers are usually not interested in private computers; they are after security holes in big Web sites. You can reduce the tiny risk of getting "hacked" by not staying online for long stretches at a time, say overnight.

Can I get a computer virus from the Internet?

Yes, computer viruses do abound online. A **virus** is a nuisance program that can infect software programs or files on your hard drive. They can cause your computer to crash (stop working unexpectedly) or they can come with a "payload" that could do anything from making it impossible to save files to erasing all the files on your hard drive! To protect your computer from viruses, most PCs come with antivirus software that starts up when you start your Windows software and runs constantly, ready to intercept any virus that comes on the scene. To be safe, don't open e-mail attachments from people you don't know or trust, especially if the attachment is a software program. If your computer didn't come with an antivirus program, you can buy software at most computer stores that detects and eliminates viruses. Be sure to go to the antivirus company's Web site often to get the latest, newest virus protection.

using an ISP

Going local has its advantages

You've probably seen advertisements in your local paper exclaiming how you can connect to the Internet—just call this number and find out how. The phone number listed is an Internet Service Provider, or ISP. These are businesses that supply Internet access to people like you and me as well as businesses. Most ISPs are local mom-and-pop operations, but some are large national or international corporations.

To find a local ISP, check your phone book under Internet Services. (If you don't see any listed in your region, then you'll need to use an online service. See page 65.) Check out the various benefits and prices of the ISPs in your area. For example, some bill you by the month, others by the year.

Most local ISPs offer local news on their welcome page. This ISP, Computer.Net in Westchester County, NY, also gives the weather.

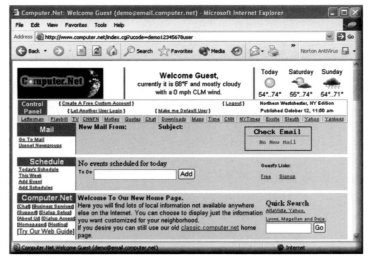

Once you've chosen your ISP, they will give you the following information so you can get started:

- First, their Internet phone number, which your computer's modem will dial into (that is called an **access phone number**). Remember to make sure this is a local number.

- Next, they will give you the Internet "address" of their computer, which is called a **domain name server** address, or DNS (usually four sets of numbers like 070.013.205.204).

- Finally, you will give them your **user name** and **password**, so think about these before you call them.

Step by step: SETTING UP YOUR ACCOUNT

1. Click on Start, All Programs, then Accessories, then Communications, then New Connection Wizard.
2. In New Connection Wizard click on the Next button. Make sure Connect to the Internet is selected and press Next again.
3. There are three options to choose from: Pick an ISP from an existing list; set up a connection manually, or install the CD-ROM you got from an ISP. Pick whichever works best for you, then click Next.
4. Depending on your choice, follow the prompts until you are done. You may need to have handy the name of your ISP server, their phone number, your user name and password.
5. When done, click the Finish button.

FIRST PERSON DISASTER

Online/Offline

All I wanted to do on my computer was be able to get online so I could check out the action on some of these auction sites. I am a collector of wines and more and more wine auctions are being held online. So I dialed up a local provider that my neighbor uses and got connected. Got all the information. Typed it all in. The DSN number, the ISP phone number, my number. You name it. When I was finished I restarted my computer, ready to start wheeling and dealing at one of the biggest wine auctions that afternoon. Nothing. Couldn't get online. Kept getting a message saying insufficient connection, try again. I kept trying and trying. I called the ISP provider and asked them what to do. We went over everything. All the numbers I had typed in were correct. So I tried again. And again. Still nothing. Needless to say, I missed the auction. Later that night, I called my ISP again to tell them to cancel my account, when they asked if I had added the number one in front of my area code and phone number. Yes, of course. "Oh, that's the problem. You don't need the number one." Oh. Swell.

Sam R., Madison, Wisconsin

using online services

Going for the big time

So you think you want to go the online services route.
It's a good way to get started using the Internet without getting too technical. Plus, many computers come with online service software already installed or at least some type of installation setup, so you're almost there.

Turn your computer and modem on and connect the modem phone line to your telephone wall jack. Windows XP makes it easy to subscribe to an online service. Click Start, All Programs, Online Services, and click on the service that you want to set up. Follow the steps and answer the questions as you go (clicking the Next button to continue through the setup).

Most likely you will be signing up for a new account. If you have any problems setting up your online service or finding an access number (which is the number your modem calls to get online), there should be some technical support numbers that you can call for help. Click the Help button on the opening screen and click through the contents to find the Member Support phone numbers.

Some online providers, such as America Online, let you access your e-mail right from their home page. See that little mailbox icon in the left-hand column? Click on it, and it will immediately take you to your e-mail account.

SK THE EXPERTS

I just got a CD in the mail from an online service promoting their software. How does that work?

The CD is basically a mini-trial of how the online service works. All you need is a phone line and a modem, and you're in business. They are giving you a free trial without setting up an account. The free trial gives you a certain number of minutes "free" online to research, send e-mail—whatever you want. To install the software from a CD, refer to "Loading Software" (pages 24–25) for help.

I live in a rural area. Is there online service for me?

The chances of finding a local service provider are probably small. You can always go with a big online service. Just make sure they have a local phone number available in your area. If the closest number they have is a long-distance one, you will run up your phone bill by paying for long-distance connections or the extra fees they often tack on to utilize a toll-free number.

I don't know which way is better, ISPs or online providers?

There are pros and cons to each one, many of which will change over time as online companies continue to improve their services. But for starters, ISPs are typically local outfits that can provide you with local service. That means anything from a home page that has local weather and movie information to easy access to a tech person to answer your tech questions. For some, local is nice; for others who work at 3 a.m. when the tech person is sleeping, it's a problem. Online providers offer national service with a slew of tech people to help you. That said, they also can suffer from online congestion because so many of their customers are trying to get online at peak hours, say 7–10 p.m. Online providers offer easy, speedy access to national news as well as national sites. Good advice: Compare prices and services before you sign up. And remember, nothing is forever. You can cancel and switch to another provider if you're not happy.

getting around the Web

You gotta use a board to surf the Net

You've got a modem and a service provider. Now what?

You need something called a **browser.** That's the computer name for software that allows you to navigate the Internet. Think of it as the surfboard that allows you to surf the Web. Happily, your computer most likely came with a browser installed; some brand names are Netscape Navigator or Microsoft's Internet Explorer. If yours doesn't have a browser, you will have to purchase browser software at your local computer store and install it (see pages 24–25).

Here's how to begin using your browser:

1. Click Start, Internet (the option near the top left) to open your browser. You may also have your browser's icon on the Desktop, which you must double-click to launch your browser.

2. When the application opens, click on the Connect button in the Dial-Up Connection box. Your modem will begin dialing and log you onto the Internet.

When your browser software opens, it will most likely open to its home page (the screen you see when you first access a Web site). It usually contains an index, search options, and connections to other Web pages. Take a look at that home page. Do you see text that is underlined? Text that is darker and underlined is called a **hyperlink** (or sometimes just link). If you click on the underlined text, it will automatically "link" you to a different page or perhaps another Web site. If you click on a link and want to go back to where you were, click on the Back button on the Web browser button bar (located at the top of your screen, beneath the browser title bar). Notice that after you have clicked on a link, it is a different color— letting you know you have been there before.

HAT IF

You want to print out a Web page?

Click the Print button on the Web browser button bar. It is at the top far right of your screen.

Your Web page doesn't display right away, and you see a page that says it didn't come up properly?

Click the Refresh button on the Web browser button bar.

You want to click on a link, but not exit the current page?

Right-click on the link and choose Open in New Window. This will open a new window along with the previous one.

You don't have an Internet Service Provider but want to get to the Internet?

You can get help from some online services. Click on Start, then on Programs, then on Online Services. You will see a list of various online providers. Select one, and it will ask you for your phone number. Then dial a toll-free number and find the best local access number for you. It will then ask for your credit card number and officially sign you up.

researching online

*Surfing the web
is as easy as
catching a wave*

The Internet continues to grow with more and more
information each day, which is stored in an abundance of
databases (computer files full of systematically arranged information). In order to find what you seek, there are companies out there
that have created user-friendly **search engines**—programs that tap
into these databases by using **keywords**, a word or words that
define your subject. Some names of popular search engines are
Yahoo, Excite, AltaVista, and Looksmart. (For a listing of search
engines see page 81.)

Here's how search engines work: If you want to look up information on puppies, you would simply type the key word *puppies* in
the Search box and click the Search button. You will then see a list
of underlined links (from news articles about puppies to sites that
sell puppy food) to choose from. Click on the particular link that
interests you, and away you go. To avoid getting a slew of links,
narrow your search. For example, type **puppy food** in the Search
box instead of just **puppy**.

Type the name of
the search engine
in your browser's
address box. Once
you finish typing,
hit the Enter key. In
a few seconds or
minutes (depend-
ing on the speed of
your modem) you
will see the search
engine's home, or
first, page—in this
case Yahoo!'s.

Browser address —

Search —
button

Search box —
(key words such as
puppies goes here)

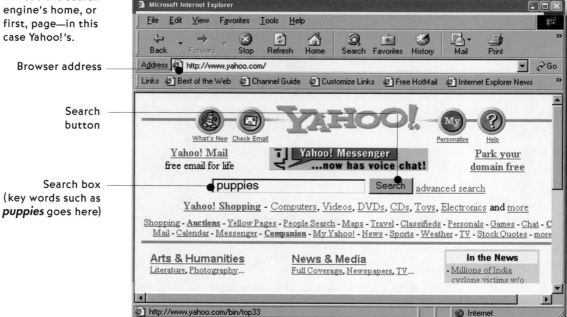

There's another way to search. You can go right to a specific site if you know its address. What is a **Web address**? It tells your computer where a company, an organization, even people (more on that later) are on the Web. Instead of using the Search box, you go up to the Address bar and type in the Web address and press Enter. You should immediately be taken to the home page of that address.

ASK THE EXPERTS

What do "http" and "www" stand for?

Get ready for a little technical lingo. HTTP stands for Hypertext Transfer Protocol. Basically, it's the code that allows you to send and receive stuff over the Web. You don't need to type in the http:// when you are browsing the Web. It will automatically do it for you. Most companies have the www. before their name, which stands for the World Wide Web. It's best to type it in the address field.

What are the slashes and dots doing in an Internet address?

The slashes and dots between words are providing specific location information about the address, a bit like a zip code.

How do I mark a Web site to come back to it again later?

Say you have found a new site that you really like. Instead of typing in its Web address every time, you can **bookmark**, or earmark, it for instant access. To bookmark a site, you must be currently looking at it. How do you bookmark? In Internet Explorer, go up to the Menu bar and choose Favorites, then Add to Favorites. The site's name will get added to your Favorites list. Next time you want that site, go up to Favorites and a list of all your added favorites will scroll down; click on your newly added site and it will instantly appear. In Netscape Navigator, you click on Bookmarks, then choose Add to Bookmarks. Next time you click on Bookmarks you'll see the name of your newly added site.

WEB ADDRESSES

A Web address is the address you type in to get to a place on the Internet. Nearly all Web addresses start with www for World Wide Web, then dot (typed as a period), then the name of the organization, then dot and an abbreviation. For instance, the Web address for Barnes & Noble is: www.bn.com. For the Public Broadcasting System: www.PBS.org. The last three letters of the address tell you something about the site.

.com a company
.org a nonprofit organization
.net a network provider
.edu school or university
.gov U.S. government
.mil the military

shopping online

No more long lines at the cash register

Ever go shopping and find a parking spot right away, walk directly to the right department, and then discover that the item you are looking for is not there? Well, those days are gone. You can shop online, find what you want, and get it mailed to you; and if the vendors don't happen to have it, they'll mail it when they do. And chances are it will be cheaper than in the store, although there will usually be an extra charge for mailing it to you. All you need is access to the Internet, a browser, and a credit card.

Just as in the real world, there are a number of different ways to shop on the Internet: 1) directly from the manufacturer such as **www.ibm.com**; 2) from retail stores like **www.bn.com**; 3) from cyberspace-only stores like **www.eToys.com**; 4) from Internet malls like **www.shopnow.com**; 5) from online auctions like **www.ebay.com**; and 6) from catalogs like **www.landsend.com**. Some things never change: When you first get to a site you can expect to see specials, sales, and a pitch—just as you would at a local store.

How do you actually shop online? Well, most sites have you put your chosen items into a "shopping cart." A link then takes you to your checkout point—where you can review your merchandise, type in who you are and where you want your merchandise sent, and enter your credit card number. It will tell you the total cost including shipping and handling. Simply type in the appropriate information and your merchandise will be sent to you within the time that the store specifies.

Instead of hunting through a store for what you want, you simply type in what you want and, presto, you see it on your computer screen. One click and it's in your virtual shopping cart.

ASK THE EXPERTS

How can I search for a particular item on a shopping site?

You can usually search for products by category, but it can be faster to use the site's search box. Type in the word(s) that describe the product, manufacturer, or type of goods, and click the Go button or Search button. Review the list of items and click on the appropriate link.

How safe is it to use my credit card online?

Don't type in your credit card number unless the site is **secure**, meaning that any information you give is **encrypted**, or coded, so that no intruder can use it. To determine if a site is secure, look for a closed padlock or unbroken key icon in the status bar along the bottom of the window. If the padlock is open, or the key is broken, the site is not secure.

Are my shopping habits ever kept track of?

Often when you buy things online, the seller puts a **cookie** into your virtual shopping cart. The cookie links your name to your purchase so the seller knows what types of goods and services you are interested in. (For more on cookies, see page 81).

(For more on cookies, see page 81).

GOOD DEALS BAD DEALS

Be wary. Just because it's online doesn't mean you are getting a deal. One thing in particular to watch for is the shipping and handling charges. You might find a site that has merchandise at a large discount, but by the time you add the shipping and handling charges, you would be paying more than you would if you went to the corner store.

auctions online

Going . . . going . . . gone!

Imagine you've got a closetful of stuff you don't use anymore. (Not too hard, is it?) Sure, you could hold a garage sale, but if you're tired of tire kickers trying to haggle you down, you can find a good home for more or less anything by holding an online auction. And once you've freed up space in that closet, you can bid on other people's unappreciated treasures to fill it up again!

Sure, dealing with strangers can be a leap of faith, but auction sites have a good self-policing system in place. Sellers and buyers build a reputation—people they do business with can leave electronic feedback about how friendly or fast a buyer or seller is. The more positive feedback you see, the more confident you can feel about doing business with someone. And if a deal goes bad, the auction site intervenes: Descriptions and bids are legally binding contracts. If there's any funny business, the auction site will usually revoke membership. Bad customers don't stick around long, so you can bid and sell with a fair amount of confidence.

There are a number of auction sites to choose from, and the list just keeps growing. For starters, check out **www.ebay.com** (shown here).

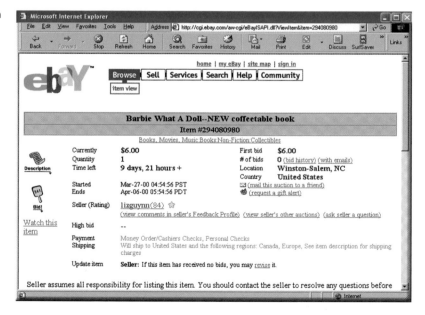

STEP BY STEP: AUCTIONING

1. Sign up with an online auction site. Click on the site's "join" link and be prepared to enter your real name, address, and e-mail address, as well as a screen name and password. If you're selling, you'll probably need to enter a credit card number or arrange to send a check to the company so that they can deduct an "insertion fee" (usually between a quarter and a dollar) for listing your item. They'll also want a percentage of the final bidding price—no more than 5 percent.

2. Once you've joined, you can put up items for sale. Sellers should set a realistic starting price (aim low to encourage bidders, but not so low that you'd be upset if you got only the opening bid). Compose an accurate description of the item (and be up-front about any faults or flaws—buyers don't like surprises). It's also helpful to find out before the auction how much it will cost to ship the item.

3. Buyers can search for items by entering key words (Pokemon, Beanie baby, Chippendale chairs, and so on) in the site's Search box. The matching list is sorted by date, with the auctions about to close at the top. If an item seems interesting, click on it.

4. When the auction closes, the auction site will send e-mail to the highest bidder and the seller. These two must figure out the details by themselves in a fixed time frame—usually a week. They work out how to pay (check, money order, or whatever), how to deliver, and do what they've agreed on. Many sellers insist on waiting until an out-of-state check clears before delivering—so the buyer may wait a few weeks after the last bid before seeing the goods.

5. When the goods arrive, it's helpful to leave a feedback message about the experience at the site. A good seller deserves praise, and other buyers deserve to know if a seller is slow or not very communicative.

BARGAIN HUNTING

Sites like **www.price-line.com** and **www.infostart.com** are places where businesses provide goods that they're prepared to sell below retail price. You, as a buyer, can search for something you want and name a price you're prepared to pay. The company can take or leave your offer, so if you don't bid too low (or if the company has over-stocked and is desperate to empty its warehouses), you can usually get a great deal.

chatting online

Connect with people who have similar interests

Ever feel like talking about your favorite hobby or local sports team, but there's no one around? If so, then Internet chat rooms may be just what you're looking for. It's a bit like instant mail. You type your comment, and someone responds with theirs. You can end up having a written conversation about everything from favorite soap operas to intergalactic space travel.

Online services have built-in chat rooms where you can talk about virtually anything with other people who share your service. If you have an ISP and are looking for a chat room using your Web browser, you can find a Chat link on most of the World Wide Web search engine sites (refer to page 81). You can also access these sites from your online service, but you need to use the Web link instead of your service's chat option.

You can choose many different topics to chat about in the free chat areas of **publicchat.msn. com**.

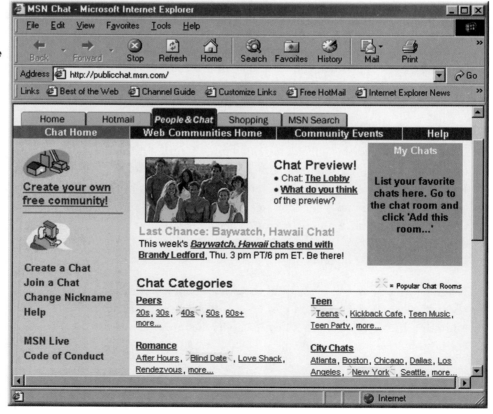

For an example of a typical online chat, try the free service available from The Microsoft Network.

1. Type chat.msn.com into the Address line, then press Enter.

2. Click the chat topic you are interested in.

3. Select a chat name (any nickname you fancy).

4. Click the connect button. You'll see chat software downloading into your Web browser window—don't panic! This is exactly what you need. When it's all installed, you'll be able to read chat messages in one chat window and type in your own comments in another. Your message is invisible until you click the Send button. Then it's posted for everyone to see.

5. To end your chat session, click the Exit this Chat button.

ASK THE EXPERTS

How do I send a message privately to one user?

You may invite someone (or they may invite you) to a **private room** if you are using an online service (or **whisper with you**—if you are using **http://chat.msn.com**), where you can talk one-on-one. To send a message to a particular user, highlight the user from the users list on the right, select the Private User option, and type your message (or type your message and click the Whisper button). Everything you type will be seen only by you and the other user until you turn the Private User option off (or stop clicking the Whisper button to send the message).

How do I screen out rude or annoying users?

To screen out obnoxious users, highlight the user from the users list on the right and select the Ignore option.

how to chat

Want to chat with someone online? Well, don't let the
word "chat" confuse you—you'll be typing messages, not talking.
And you'll both need to download and install a chat program and
be online at the same time. But apart from that, it's all pretty easy.
If you want to chat with people who use the America Online service as well as with people on the Internet at large, your best bet is
to get America Online's Instant Messenger program, also known as
AIM. Don't worry—it's free, and you don't need to subscribe to the
company's online service to use it.

1. Go to **www.aol.com** to download the AIM program to your desktop. An icon of the AIM program will appear on your desktop.
   Double-click on it and it will open.

2. AIM will ask you to pick a screen name and password. The
   screen name you pick will appear on all the messages you type.
   Make a note of it and pass it around to your friends as your new
   AOL/AIM identification. And get their screen names too.

3. Every time you get online, AIM will start up and let your buddies know that you're available for a chat.

4. To see whether your buddies are online, add them to your
   "Buddy List"—all you need to know is their screen names. In
   AIM's Buddy List window, click on the List Setup tab and right-
   click on Buddies. Select Add Buddy and type in your buddy's
   screen name. Then click on the Online tab.

5. If your friend is online, you'll see his or her name in the Buddy
   List window. Double-click on it. A new window will appear. Type
   a quick greeting and press the Enter key.

6. When your friend sees you're starting a chat, he or she will send
   a reply. Don't be impatient—they may be away from their computer when you first say "hi." You can then hold a "conversation"
   by typing messages and hitting the Enter key to send them.

caroline - Instant Message

File   Edit   Insert   People   carolinelW's Warning Level: 0%

Hector: Got a minute?
Hector: What did you want to do for dinner?
caroline: I thought we could sacrifice one of the goats.
Hector: I was thinking more along the lines of
Italian. I think there's a good one around the
neighborhood somewhere

A A   A A A   B I U   link

Warn Block   Add Buddy   Talk   Get Info   Send

now what do I do?

Answers to common problems

What does it mean when the computer says "Click here to download this file?"

Downloading is transferring a file, that is, copying it from the large group of computers that make up the Internet onto your computer's hard drive using your modem. You can download games, research information, or a program that will help your computer accomplish a specific task. Note that the larger the file, the longer it takes to download. So you have to have patience . . . or a really fast Internet connection.

Where can I get help getting online?

If you want help with getting connected to the Internet, click Start, Connect to, and it will show you a list of any Internet connection you have set up.

What do I do if I have call waiting on my regular phone line?

Call waiting will cause static on your Internet connection, which will most likely disconnect you. So before you go online, click on the Dialing Properties button in the Modem Properties dialogue box to modify how your calls are dialed.

Where do I get help if my modem is giving me trouble?

Click Start, point to Help, type "modem" into the Help window keyword box, click the Display button, and then double-click on Troubleshooting Modems in the Suggested Topics list. Click the Click Here link to begin the troubleshooter. Click the circle(s) to the left of the description of your problem. It may take a while, but Windows will help you figure out what is wrong with your modem. It might not be your modem at all. It might be your individual online connection settings.

What does it mean when a message says "The page cannot be displayed?"

It could mean a couple of things. First, you might have typed in the Web address incorrectly; check it again to be sure. Second, the Web site might not exist, so you need to check the address that you are trying to type in. Third, if you received this message after clicking on a Web hyperlink, there might be something temporarily wrong with the site's Web server, so click the Refresh button on your Web browser and see if it works. If this doesn't work, simply try the link later.

Why do I sometimes get a busy signal when I try to connect to the Internet?

Most likely, your Internet Service Provider or online service has too many people trying to use it at the same time. This is similar to when you call a friend and their line is busy. It means someone is already using the phone line and you need to wait until someone hangs up. Just keep trying or try some of the different numbers your service gave you to dial in. If this is a persistent problem, contact your service and see how they can help you resolve this problem.

Do manufacturers get information about me from what I buy?

Yes. It's called a cookie. A cookie is a small file that some Web sites insert onto your hard drive when you visit them for the first time. The information stored in the cookie enables that site to compile information about your browsing habits and purchases to help them serve you better. They can also pass this information on to other Web sites. Virtual shopping carts need cookies to complete your on line order.

What are some of the most popular search engines?

AltaVista	**www.altavista.com**
Excite	**www.excite.com**
Google	**www.google.com**
GoTo	**www.goto.com**
HotBot	**www.hotbot.com**
InfoSeek	**www.infoseek.com**
Lycos	**www.lycos.com**
Yahoo!	**www.yahoo.com**
Looksmart	**www.looksmart.com**

HELPFUL RESOURCES

CONTACTS	BOOKS
Netscape Navigator (800) 411-0707 (A credit card is required; the charge is $29 per incident, a.k.a. problem.)	**America Online for Dummies** By John Kaufeld
America Online (888) 346-3704	**Ebay for Dummies** By Roland Woerner
Internet Explorer for Win 9x (425) 635-7123	**Internet Auctions for Dummies** By Greg Holden

E-mail

4

All you really want to do is e-mail the family, maybe some friends. It's why you bought the book, right? So learn how easy it is to get an e-mail account. How to receive and send messages and attachments. It's fun. The days of letters and stamps are over.

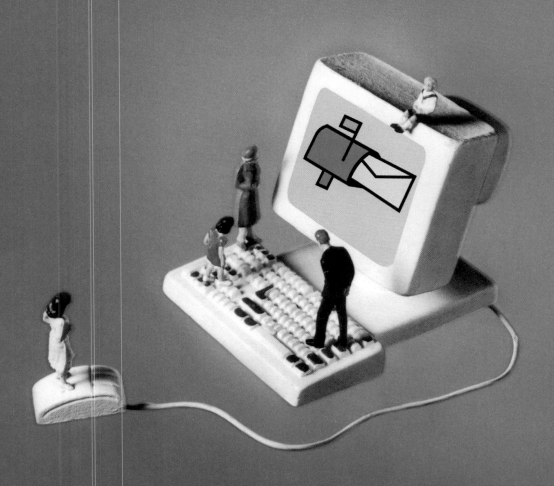

getting an e-mail account

It's just like having your own mailbox in cyberspace

Let's be frank. The real reason for signing up with your friendly Internet Service Provider or online service is to get an **e-mail** account. E-mail is computerspeak for electronic mail. This is where you send and receive letters, messages, or even greeting cards complete with interactive videos. There are millions of folks who also have e-mail accounts. There's a good chance some of them are your friends and family.

Once you've gotten your online service set up (see pages 64–67), your provider will offer you an e-mail account. As with everything else in computerland, you need software. **Online software** can be tucked into your **browser software** (the software that lets you use the Internet), or it might be part of your operating system software (see pages 68–69). For example, if you use the Netscape browser, you might use Netscape Messenger, or you might use Outlook Express, which comes with your Windows operating system.

See that mailbox with a letter sticking out? That's your electronic mailbox. You've got mail. Click on it and find out from whom.

You could also use Eudora Light or Pegasus, both of which are popular e-mail programs for the Internet. (It's a good idea to check with your online provider to see if they have a specific e-mail program they recommend or want you to use and if it costs extra.)

Some providers let you sign up for free e-mail software. Yes, FREE! Some popular companies are Juno at **www.juno.com** and Freeinet at **www.freei.net**. To use their e-mail software, you have to download it from the Internet. (See page 80 to download.) The only drawback to free e-mail is that you will get a lot of electronic advertisements.

SK THE EXPERTS

How safe is e-mail?

Keep in mind that e-mail messages are like electronic postcards. Other people can sometimes gain access and read them. The real problem with e-mail is not prying eyes, but computer **viruses**. These are man-made computer bugs that are spread via e-mail, (see page 63 for more info on viruses). If you open an infected e-mail, it can sometimes wreak havoc with your computer. Do not open e-mail messages from people or companies you do not know.

How can companies afford to offer free e-mail?

Advertising is the name of the game. Have you seen those little blinking advertisements that appear on-screen when using your Web browser? Each time you click on one of those blinking advertisements—known as **banners**—you are being tracked (see pages 25, 73, and 81 for more information on cookies). If you end up buying something from a Web site that the banner "led" you to, that advertiser gets the credit. Banner advertisements are tailored to your specific interests and purchasing habits. When you sign up for free e-mail, be prepared to see a lot of banners.

your e-mail address

No more waiting in line at the post office

When you send e-mail, you follow all the similar actions of writing a letter: writing it, addressing it, and placing it in a mailbox—except all these actions are now done on your computer screen in a fraction of the time. Welcome to the millennium.

Before you can send or receive anything, you need to have an address. Your Internet—rather, your e-mail—address is made up of two parts: your name (some people use their real names; others make up names), and your domain name—technospeak for the name of your e-mail provider, for example, AOL or the Microsoft Network. Note this: These two parts are separated by an @, or "at," sign. For example, here's a typical e-mail address: MaryPrankster@aol.com. Let's decipher it: MaryPrankster is the person's log-on name, and her e-mail account is at the America Online Company, or to use its domain name, aol.com. (Remember ".com" is Internet shorthand for company.) Or in the following address, julie@pets.org, for example, the first part, julie, is the log-on name (like a home address) and pets.org is the domain name. (.org is computer shorthand for a nonprofit organization.)

To send e-mail, you must know the exact Internet address, just as you must know the right address to put on an envelope going through the U.S. mail. The Internet is composed of computers that are linked all over the globe, and each one acts as a post office to route your message to the right destination.

Here's the trade-off: regular mail vs. e-mail. The good old U.S. mail is so slow in comparison to e-mail, it is called snail mail. Then again, snail mail costs only the price of a stamp; e-mail requires a monthly fee. Alas, modern living now calls for using both.

ASK THE EXPERTS

What happens if I get part of an e-mail address wrong?

If you get any part of an e-mail address wrong and send it, it will be returned to you with an error message saying your intended recipient couldn't be found (so you will know to recheck the e-mail address).

Why do some people use lowercase letters in their e-mail addresses?

E-mail addresses are not case sensitive. The computer will read a capital letter or a lowercase letter the same way, so don't worry about whether you should capitalize a name or not.

Can I just have letters and numbers in my e-mail address, or can I use other characters?

The only other allowable characters in an e-mail address are periods, underscores, and hyphens. For example, mary.prankster; mary_prankster; or mary-prankster. You can't use ampersands (&), slashes (/), or asterisks (*).

LOST AND FOUND

If you want to find the e-mail address of a friend that you have lost touch with, you can use the popular Internet Address Finder, which contains around 6 million addresses. You can access this information at www.iaf.net by first adding your e-mail address to the list of names. This will help other people find you as well. There are many address locators. Here are a few others you can check: **www.whowhere.com, www.bigfoot.com,** and **people.yahoo.com** (no www. needed).

getting e-mail messages

Finally, you've got mail!

Okay. You've signed up and gotten an e-mail account. Chances are your very first message will be from your online account to check that all is well. New messages are received in the Inbox of your e-mail program (think of it as your new inbox on your desk). New, unread messages are usually displayed in bold type. Messages you have already read are usually in regular type.

In some programs, when you click the mouse pointer on a new-message line, you will be able to view the message on your computer screen, usually in some sort of box format. In other programs, you need to double-click on the message to open it into its own window. When you have finished reading your messages, you can usually close, delete, or send them to someone else (see "Sending e-mail" on page 90). Otherwise they will automatically be stored in your inbox mail file.

Here's a typical e-mail box. It tells you who the e-mail is from, the subject, and the date and time it was received. Notice how some e-mails have a paper clip next to them. That means an electronic file (or document) is attached along with it. (See next page.)

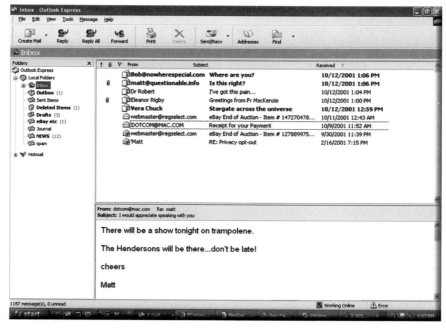

ASK THE EXPERTS

How do I reply directly to a message?

Once you open and read a message, you will probably want to reply to it. You can reply to the person who sent you the message (known as the **sender**) by clicking on Reply or Reply to All (if there was more than one recipient).

How do I open an e-mail attachment?

If you see a paper clip or some other symbol next to an e-mail in your inbox, that means it has an **attachment** to it. When you open your message, you should see an icon, a stamp-sized box with text describing the attached file. To open the attachment, double-click on it. If it doesn't open, you probably don't have the right software to read the file. E-mail a message back to the sender asking how to open it and what software program the file is written in. If there is a **.zip** after the file name, that means it's been **compressed** so it can be **downloaded**, or copied from the Internet, more quickly . To expand it back to normal, you need software called Winzip, which is available at most computer stores.

YOUR E-MAIL ADDRESS BOOK

When writing an e-mail, use the address book to select recipients without having to type their entire e-mail address in the field. Each browswer has a different way of adding and using addresses. To start your address book, click on the Address link or icon. A box will open; type in the name and e-mail address of friends and family. To use this time-saving feature, start a new message, then click on the To: button and select a name from the address book.

FIRST PERSON DISASTER

E-Mailer Beware

I love my computer. It's made time-consuming tasks like writing letters to friends and family easy. I used to write these long letters, now I just e-mail away and bing off it goes. It's amazing. (I wonder if this is how my grandmother felt when she took her first ride in a Ford Model T.) The only bad thing is that I get a lot of unsolicited e-mail—mostly from people wanting to sell me stuff. But there was one e-mail I'll never forget. It said it was from a discount travel agency. If I opened up the link (the underlined part) in the e-mail message, it would link me to a super discount site for Hawaii. Of course, I did just that. Instead of Hawaii, it kept repeating the message over and over again and I couldn't stop it. Even when I turned off my computer and restarted it, the message was still there. I was so unnerved I called my service provider, who told me that the link to the discount site had a virus which had attacked my computer. They suggested I buy antivirus software and install it and it would kill the virus. I did and was back up and running. The moral: don't open any links from any e-mailer you don't know. It's just like my grandmother used to tell us kids, don't get in a car with a stranger.

Molly G., Darien, Connecticut

sending e-mail

When you click on your e-mail icon, it will automatically set up a page to write an e-mail. It will justify the margins and pick the font size, much like a word processing letter (see page 48). You can view and compose your e-mail messages by using the following features:

A Print command icon: Use it to print a copy of an e-mail before or after you send it, or print a copy of a received e-mail.

B Send To box: Type the name or address of your e-mail recipient here.

C Copy To box: Use it to forward copies of an e-mail you are about to send.

D Subject box: Use it to give your e-mail a name or title (a must with most e-mail software).

E E-mail tool bar: Use it to change your e-mail style defaults.

F E-mail letter window: Type your e-mail message here.

G Attachments button: Click on it if you want to include an attachment with your message. An Attachment dialogue box will open. Click on Attach, which brings up another dialogue box with all your files listed. Find the file you want to attach and double-click on it. It will be added to your attachment box. Click OK. You will see a floppy-disk icon of the file in your e-mail message.

Send Now

Send Now icon: When your e-mail is ready to send off, click on it.

Send Later

Send Later icon: Click on it when you want to delay sending your e-mail.

sending attachments

Share your pictures the e-mail way

Your computer's hard drive is probably a treasure chest of cool things—ranging from digital pictures of your pets to that first draft of the Great American Novel you've been working on. If you want to share any of the stuff you have there, then e-mail is a great way to do it.

And it's easy to do too. When you're composing an e-mail message, check out the tool bar at the top of your software for a paper clip icon, or look for some other button labeled Attach or Attachment. Almost all e-mail software has one—even Web-based e-mail services such as HotMail and YahooMail.

STEP BY STEP: SENDING ATTACHMENTS

1. When you click on the Attach button, a dialogue box appears.

2. Check out the drives on your hard disk, and click on the one that contains the file. (The drive labeled C: will be your hard disk, where most of your files are stored.)

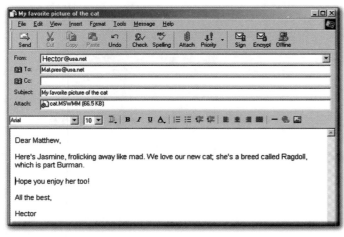

3. Look for the folder in which your file is stored, and open it by double-clicking it.

4. When you find the file you want to share, double-click on its icon. Click on OK if the dialogue box is still open.

5. You'll be returned to the message you're writing, but you'll see a new element on the screen—the name of the file you just attached (and how much memory it takes up).

6. If the wrong file is listed, you probably misclicked in step 4. No problem—just right-click on the attachment, select Delete from the drop-down menu that appears, and start again.

That's all. When you send the e-mail, the attachment will go with it.

ASK THE EXPERTS

Why does it take so long to send an e-mail attachment?

The bigger the attachment, the longer it takes to to send. And anything larger than 2 megabytes (about the size of two 8x10-inch digital photographs) won't go through at all. The smaller the attachment, the faster it goes to the sender.

I have to send a big file! What can I do?

Your only choice is to **compress** the file you have. If you have Windows 95, 98, or 2000, you will need to download a software program called WinZip (see page 105 for information about downloading). This program will both compress files for easy mailing and decompress them back to normal size for viewing. You can also buy it at your computer or office supply store.

To compress a file, you need first to select the file, then right-click on it (use the *right* button on the mouse). A menu bar will come down. Choose Add to Zip, then follow the WinZip directions. To open a compressed file, you simply click on it and drag it to your desktop, then double-click to open it. (It will uncompress on the way to your desktop.)

If you have Windows Millennium Edition (Windows ME to its friends), you have something like WinZip built in. To use it while you are in your e-mail program, click on the attachment paper clip and find the file you want to attach. Then use the *right* mouse button to click on it and select Send To. Click on the option Compressed Folder, and Windows will shrink the file down into what looks like a folder, but which is actually a file with the same name but with the extension .zip. Now click the Attach button.

now what do I do?

Answers to common problems

Someone wrote 'BFN' in an e-mail to me. What does this mean?

'BFN' means Bye for now. There are many common initializations used in e-mail because they take up so much less space than writing out the phrase. Here are some others:

ATB	All the best	IMO	In my opinion
BFN	Bye for now	LOL	Laughing out loud
BTW	By the way	OTF	On the floor (laughing)
FWIW	For what it's worth	TIA	Thanks in advance
FYI	For your information	TTFN	Ta Ta for now
IMHO	In my humble opinion	TTYL	Talk to you later

How do I e-mail the same group of people?

Groups are lists of e-mail addresses that you can create when there is a particular set of people you regularly want e-mail messages to go to. For example, if you like sending jokes to all your friends, you might want to create a Jokes group that contains all the e-mail addresses of your friends. In your address book, simply click the New Group option and select the names or type the addresses of the people you want in the group. Then, when you want to send a message to all those people, you only have to click on the group name, not each individual e-mail address.

What do some of the smiley faces mean in e-mail messages?

The following are a few known emoticons, which are "emotions" + "icons:"

:-)	A smile	;-)	A wink
8-)	Goofy smile—or glasses	:-&	Tongue-tied
:-(	Sadness, disapproval	:-p	Tongue stuck out

How can I have my computer tell me when I get an e-mail?

When you are online, depending on your e-mail program, new messages might pop up automatically. If not, you will have to click the Send/Receive button on the button bar.

What happens to e-mail messages when I delete them?

Each e-mail program treats read E-mails differently. Click once to highlight the e-mail message line in your Inbox and press the Delete key on the keyboard. Depending on your e-mail program, your message will either be gone for good or remain temporarily in a Deleted Items folder (similar to the Windows Recycle Bin) waiting for you to right-click and empty the bin for good.

How can I forward a message to someone else?

Sometimes when you read an e-mail message, you may want to forward it to another person. For example, you receive a funny joke from your aunt and want your best friend to read it as well. In that case, you can forward the message to that person. When you click the Forward button, the message will usually remain at the bottom of the e-mail—unless you have instructed your e-mail not to do that in the preferences area. Then, fill out the new-message box just as you would a new message. Try to add a sentence or two that explains why you're forwarding the message.

HELPFUL RESOURCES

CONTACTS	BOOKS
Microsoft Outlook Express (425) 635-7056	**E-mail for Dummies** By John B. Levine
Netscape Mail (800) 411-0707 (A credit card is required; the charge is $29 per incident, a.k.a. problem.)	
America Online (888) 346-3704	

Pictures

5

Pictures are worth a thousand words.
That's because they usually cost a bundle.
In this chapter you'll learn how to use art from the
Internet and pop it into letters. You'll see how easy it is
to insert pictures you've drawn yourself or photos
you've scanned in.

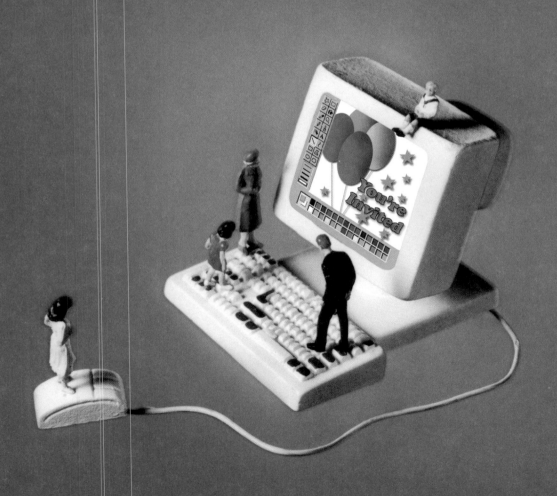

adding pictures to a letter

Relax. It's so easy to pop a picture in

It's true. You can add a picture, photo, or drawing to any of your letters. How is this amazing feat done? Nearly all word processing software comes with a mini-collection of **graphics—** that's techspeak for pictures.

For home use, most word processing programs (Microsoft Word, Corel WordPerfect, or WordPro) come with graphics files, and it's easy to insert them into your letter. Where do these graphics come from? Well, most come from stock photo agencies. They keep tabs on graphics—also called **clip art** by the in-the-know people. These bits of clip art are tucked away in a folder in your software program. (To insert them, see the next page.) If you feel daring, you can use your own photos or drawings (more on how to do that later in the chapter).

Why add a picture? As any magazine editor will tell you, the judicious use of a picture can cut your writing time in half.

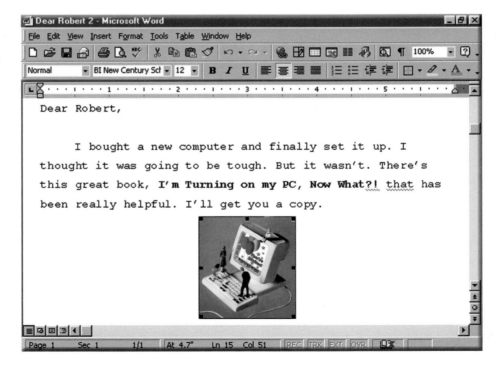

STEP BY STEP: INSERTING CLIP ART

1. In Microsoft Word, for example, open up the document into which you want to insert a picture. Use the mouse and click in the text where you want the picture to go. Leave the document open.

2. Now go up to the Menu bar and click Insert.

3. Go down to Picture and hold the mouse button down. This will open a **submenu** (a menu within in a bigger menu) that will allow you to insert Clip Art or a picture. Choose Clip Art and let go of the mouse button.

4. A dialogue box will appear with a list of Clip Art categories. Choose a category and click on it. Look through the Clip Art choices in that category. (If you don't like them, go to the Web. See page 104.)

5. Choose a picture by clicking on it once. You'll see an Insert button—click on it. The picture will appear in your document and the Clip Art box will close.

WHAT IF

You want to change the size of a graphic once it is in your letter?

Click once on the picture, and you'll see a box with tabs surrounding the art. Hold the mouse pointer over one of the corner tabs and click and drag to make the picture smaller or larger. To make the picture wider, click and drag on a side tab; to make it taller, click and drag on a top or bottom tab. Notice, though, that using side, top, and bottom tabs may distort your picture.

You want to move the picture?

Move the mouse pointer somewhere in the middle of the picture and click. The cursor may change to a cross that looks like the points of a compass, or you'll get a little dotted-outline box that moves. Click and drag the mouse, and the whole picture will move where you drag it. To delete it entirely, click on the picture and press the Delete key on the keyboard.

BLACK AND WHITE OR COLOR

If you have a black-and-white printer, then all your graphics—colored or not—will print in gray tones. If you want to print your pictures in color, purchase a good color ink-jet printer for about $150 to $200.

drawing pictures

You don't even have to draw very well to turn out a computer picture

Yes, Virginia, you can draw a picture on your computer!
Granted, it won't turn your creations into Rembrandts, but a computer can turn even the most untalented into inspired artists. All Windows PCs come with two graphics programs—Paint and Kodak Imaging for Windows.

If you want to draw your own pictures, or edit someone else's, try Paint. This program can do all sorts of things—draw lines and shapes, spray color like an airbrush, fill in the background instantly with a solid block of color. Once you're done, you can save the picture as a document, paste it into another document, or even save it onto your Windows desktop as wallpaper.

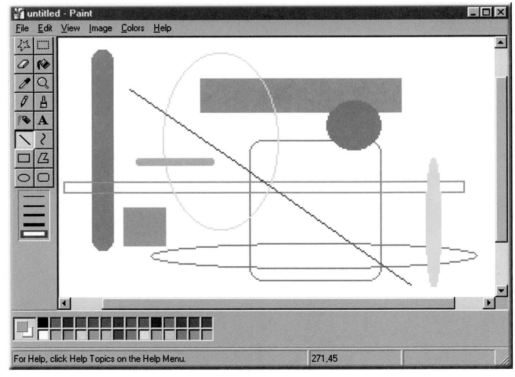

Homemade is still best-made.
This creation was drawn in
Windows' Paint program.

Picture Unperfect

It all seemed so easy. My friend e-mailed me the perfect pictures for my art history paper. She said all I had to do was click on the e-mail attachment and they would be ready to put in my report. So I clicked on the icon and got a message asking what program I wanted to open the *vangogh.sit* file with. How should I know? I called my friend and she said the *.sit* meant that the file was compressed to make it quicker to download. She said I needed software to expand it. She said she used Stuffit, but it was for Macs and won't work on a PC. Great. So much for my academic career. A week later I ran into my friend, who said she found out that there was a PC program called WinZip that could open my file. Too late, I said. I'd already handed in my paper. My teacher marked me down a grade because the paper needed examples of the artist's work.

Jamie C., Poughkeepsie, New York

STEP BY STEP: DRAWING PICTURES

1. Go to the Start menu, choose Programs, then Accessories, and click on Paint.

2. You should see a blank page (or canvas, if you will) and a toolbox of buttons on the left side of the window. You can click on any of the tools, for example, Lines, Curves, Rectangles, Polygons, Ellipses, or Rounded Rectangles.

3. First click on a color in the color palette at the bottom, choose the shape's color, then click on the line or shape you want.

4. To save the picture, choose Save from the File menu. Click the folders to choose the file location, and give the file a name you will remember, then click the Save button. To create a new picture, choose New from the File menu and start all over again.

5. To insert the picture into a document, open up the document you want and click in the text where you want it to go. Next, go up to the Menu bar and click Insert. Go down to Picture and hold, go to From File and click. Find the file that contains your drawing and either double-click it or single-click and press the Insert button on the dialogue box.

GREETING CARD EXPRESS

To create a greeting card in a Paint program, use the "line" tool and divide the canvas into quarters and create your design in the bottom right quadrant. This way, when you fold the paper into quarters, your design will be on the front. To write your greeting, use the "type" button on the tool bar—the one with the large A on it.

Too overwhelming? Turn to the Web and go to a greeting card Web site, such as **www.bluemountain.com**. Choose a card, then just type in the person's name and your message. The Web site will e-mail it for you.

your drawing desktop

In Microsoft Paint software, click on one of the boxes in the tool bar, and your mouse pointer will change shape and act like different kinds of art supplies. Any tool that draws something in your picture will use the color you click on in the color palette at the bottom of the screen. To change color, just click on a new color in the palette and it becomes the "active" color.

A Selection tools: Click on either of these tools and you can draw a box around part of a picture to copy, click and drag, or delete it. Use the star-shaped tool to select odd-shaped articles, and the rectangular tool to draw box-shaped selections.

B Eraser: Click this tool and drag the cursor across part of your picture to erase errors.

C Paint can: Select a color from the color bar. When you click on a color in the picture, the paint can will spill the new color to replace the old one.

D Dropper: If you see a color in part of a picture that you want to paint somewhere else, click on the dropper, then click on the color you like in the picture. This color will become the "active" color that will appear next time you paint.

E Magnifying glass: Click this tool, and beneath the toolbox you'll see 1x, 2x, 6x, and 8x options. These are levels of magnification to which you can blow up your image for clearer viewing. To restore, click the tool again and select 1x.

F Pencil: For drawing freehand lines, click on this tool, and then click on a color you want the pencil's virtual lead to be.

G Paintbrush: Click on this tool, and underneath the tool bar you'll see a variety of brush shapes. Pick one, click on a color, and paint.

H Spray can: The spray can comes with three levels of "spread." Click one of the splatters of paint underneath the tool bar. Then select a color and unleash your inner graffiti artist.

I A The text tool bar lets you use the keyboard to type letters into your picture. Click on it, then pick one of the options beneath the tool bar. The top picture frames any text you type in a box on top of the picture; the bottom one puts the text right into the picture. Choose a type and size in the font boxes. Then drag a box to fill with text.

J Line Tools: These two tools enable you to draw lines in five different thicknesses. Both draw straight lines, but if you select the curvy-line tool, you can click on the line after you've drawn it and drag it into smooth curves.

K Shape tools: The rectangle, rounded-edge rectangle, polygon, or oval tools let you draw a filled or open shape right in your picture. Click on one and select one of the three settings that appear under the tool bar. The top one draws open shapes; the bottom one, filled shapes; and the middle one, shapes filled with the active color with a frame in the secondary color.

using Web images

The Web is full of images you can use. Some are free, some are not

Yet another thing the Web is good for: clip art. There are many sites on the Web where you can find pictures, photos, drawings. How do you get a particular picture into your computer and onto your letter or document? It's not as hard as you think. Honest. All you need to do is click on the picture and then save it to your hard drive on your computer. This is called **downloading**. Think of it as making a copy of the picture you want and storing it in your computer. Most Web clip art is free, but some sites charge a fee for images and will ask for your credit card number before you can download. One site in particular, **www.clipart.com,** acts as a clearinghouse for a number of clip art Web sites. Images from some free clip art Web sites are for personal use only. Always read the fine print before using.

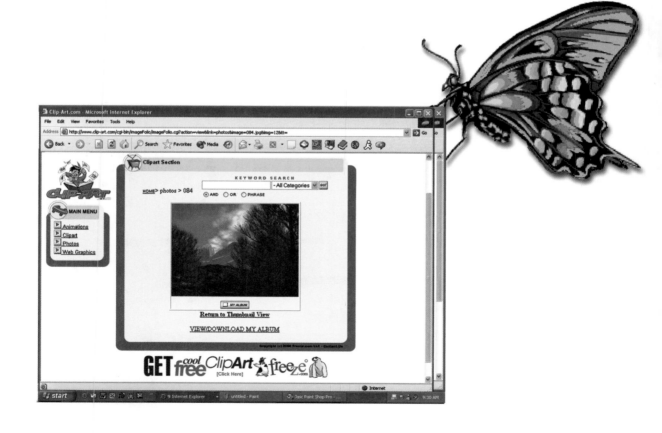

STEP BY STEP: DOWNLOADING

1. At a clip art Web site, click on the image you want to download, and the File Download dialogue box appears.

2. Click the Save this Program to Disk option and click the OK button.

3. Then indicate where you want to save the file on your hard drive and click the Save button. You will then see a dialogue box
   giving you the download information—that is, how the download is going, how long it will take, and when it is complete. (The faster your modem, the faster it will be to download images.)

4. To insert the picture you've downloaded from the Web, first open up the document in which you want to place it and click in the text where you want it to go. Next, go up to the Menu bar and click Insert. Go down to Picture and hold, go to From File and click. Find the file that contains your picture and click on it. Click the Insert button, and presto, your picture should be in your document.

ASK THE EXPERTS

What happens if I get disconnected during the download?

If you have any problems when downloading files, such as getting disconnected, or if you accidentally click the Cancel button, simply try the download again.

What if I am asked for my credit card number?

If the Web site specifies that you need to purchase a file before you download it, you might be asked to give your credit card number. Make sure you are on a secure site—you will see a little padlock or key icon in the window status bar if it is secure.

ON-LINE PHOTO DEVELOPMENT

You can also use the Web to develop your rolls of regular film into digital pictures (meaning pictures that are converted into computer files). Simply mail (as in U.S. mail) your roll of film to an online film developing company. They will process your film. Then the pictures will be scanned and **uploaded** (stored at a secure area on the Internet accessible by an access code). The company will e-mail you that your pictures are ready, and after you have paid by credit card, they will tell you where your pictures are and give you the code to **download** them to your computer. Check out **www.photonet.com** and give it a try.

scanning pictures

Put a photo of your family in your next letter

Want to insert pictures of the kids? Your scorecard from the time you broke 100 on the golf course? That adorable smile of your first grandchild? It's easy to do with something called a **scanner,** a device that looks a lot like a home photocopy machine. A scanner will copy your picture electronically, meaning that it converts it into a computer file that you can store in your computer. How exactly is it done? Well, after the image is placed on the scanner surface and the light hits or passes through it, the image is converted into computer code and stored as a digital file in your computer. Computer folk refer to this image as the **scanned image**.

There are many different types of scanners, but **flatbed** scanners are the best for home use and the least expensive. You can buy a scanner at most computer stores. Scanners scan whatever you want, color or black and white. Key point: You can print out a color picture only if you have a color printer; if you have a **monochrome** printer (techspeak for black and white), your color picture will print out in black and white.

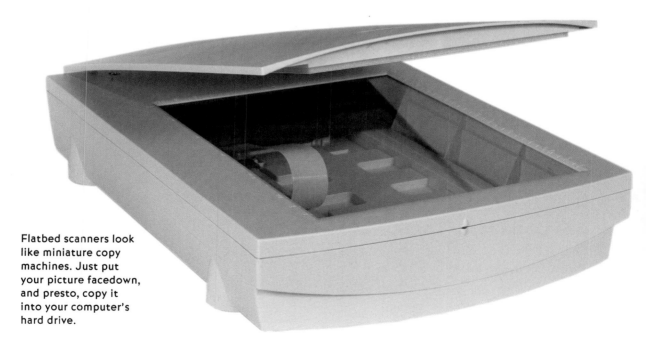

Flatbed scanners look like miniature copy machines. Just put your picture facedown, and presto, copy it into your computer's hard drive.

STEP BY STEP: SCANNING

1. Turn on the scanner.

2. Turn on your computer.

3. Raise the scanner lid.

4. Place the picture to be scanned facedown on the glass and close the lid. Take care not to scratch the glass.

5. From the Start menu, open the scanner software application on your computer. This assumes that you have already installed the software. (If you haven't, take a look at page 24 to help you install it.)

6. Tell the scanner what type of original art you are scanning by choosing **reflective** for photographs or **transparency** for slides.

7. Choose a Mode by selecting **line** for a black-and-white scan (no shades of gray), or select **grayscale** if you want shades of gray in your scan.

8. Choose a **resolution**: 72 dpi (low resolution, minimum detail), 150-300 dpi (better detail, but larger file).

9. Choose a size: 100% is the default.

10. Click **Preview**. If you like what you see, click **Scan**.

11. Click Save. You will be asked to choose a file format (don't worry—we'll explain this) and the destination, usually a folder on your hard drive. A photo can then be opened with the Imaging program under Accessories on the Start menu.

Now a quick word about file **formats**—a technical term for how the art is stored. Your computer will offer you a lot of formats to choose from, but the best choice is **JPEG** for photographs and **GIF** for other color graphics. That's because most Windows programs and Web browsers can open these formats—and that's the important thing. And don't waste a minute wondering what those terms refer to!

digital cameras

Have your computer instantly develop your photographs

Want to go direct from what you see to your computer screen? Get a digital camera. Yes, it's a little daunting, but remember that you were probably nervous when you first used a regular camera too! Digital cameras can be just as easy to use as regular point-and-shoot cameras—more so if you hate messing with rolls of film. That's right. No rolls of film. Images are stored on little memory cards inside the digital camera; then, using a cable that you connect to your computer, transferred over to your computer's hard drive.

The only real difference between a "real" camera and a digital one is that you need to choose the **picture quality** before you shoot. (Quality means how detailed and sharp your picture will look when it's printed out in a larger size). Most digital cameras provide two or three choices of picture quality. The lowest quality choices are usually fine for looking at on-screen, but if you want to print out your pictures later, you'll want the top quality setting. The trouble is, the better the quality setting you pick, the fewer pictures you can fit in the camera. That's because digital cameras work by

A nifty feature of most digital cameras is a display of the picture you just took. So if you don't like it, you can reshoot.

storing pictures on little electronic memory cards. Better pictures take up more memory. But your camera can tell you how many pictures you can fit at each quality level. Feel free to mix and match different photo quality levels. After you've transferred your pictures to your computer (see next page) you can erase the pictures from your camera's memory card and take more pictures.

DIGITAL CAMERA REVIEW

Want to learn more about digital cameras? Check out **www.pcphotoreview.com**. You will find product reviews, advice from technical experts, and specifications that will let you compare digital cameras by price and features.

STEP BY STEP: FROM CAMERA TO PC

1. First, take your pictures.

2. Plug the camera's serial or USB cable into the camera at one end and the PC at the other.

3. The camera's control program will usually start automatically. If it doesn't, double-click to open My Computer and then double-click on your camera's icon.

4. Click on the camera task instruction "Get pictures from camera."

5. You'll see another of those software Wizards called the Scanner and Camera Wizard. Click on the Next button, and you'll see lots of tiny pictures appear—they're called **thumbnails** because they're so small.

6. Click on the Next button, and you'll see two places to type stuff in: The first is a name for the group of pictures on the camera (just stick with the word that's there, Picture, if you like). The second is the folder on the hard drive where you want to store the pictures. Click Next again.

7. Once you've got the pictures on your PC, feel free to select the thumbnails in your camera control software and delete them from the camera. This frees up memory to take more pictures later.

now what do I do?

Answers to common problems

When I put pictures in my word processing documents, why do they move around?

Your word processing program is designed to move things around—that's why you can click in the middle of a sentence, type in a few words, and watch the end of the sentence move to the right as you type. Your software is designed to shift any object when you add something in front of it or apply some formatting change. If you don't like this, click in the middle of the picture until a frame of little black squares appears and drag it somewhere behind the text you're typing. Once you've finished typing, firmly affix your picture to an exact spot in your document by clicking on it and dragging it where you want it.

When I draw my own pictures, why can't I move shapes around?

Paint programs are designed to work like real painting—you can paint, draw, or stick things onto the canvas, but once it's on, it stays on until you cut it out. Luckily, with computers you can cut elements out and stick them somewhere else without making any nasty holes in your canvas. That's what the selection tools are there for, right at the top of the toolbox bar on the left of Paint's screen. You use them to draw boxes or free-form shapes around objects in your picture; then you can press the Delete key to remove them, or click and drag them somewhere else on your canvas. If you like an object so much that you want lots of it, select the Edit menu's Copy option to hide a copy of it in Windows' Clipboard, then Select Edit, then Paste. Drag the new image where you want it.

Can I resize the image I see?

Yes, you can decrease or increase the size of your image. It's called **scaling**. Go into the dialogue box of your scanner software. You'll see a dialogue box for scale. One hundred percent is the standard, meaning your scanner will scan the image at whatever size it is, e.g., 4x5- or 8x10-inch. If you want to decrease the size, type in 50%; to double its size, put in 200%, but the image will be fuzzy.

When I reply to e-mails, the whole text of the original message appears in my reply. Do attachments stay with replies too?

They don't—so don't panic about sending great big attachments back and forth. If you do want to send an e-mail complete with attachment, then forward it instead. Click on the Forward or Forward Message icon and type the e-mail address of the recipient into the Send To: Box.

When I scan my images, where does the software save them?

Most software lets you choose a name and a folder to save your files. If you accidentally saved a file but don't know where the program put it, don't panic! There are a few tricks for finding it. If the scanning software is still open, select the File menu and click on Save As. In the Save As dialogue box, check out the Save In box—that's the folder the program saved the file to. You might need to click on the little down arrow next to the folder's name to see where the folder is.

What quality pictures can I take with a consumer digital camera?

It depends on the camera and the quality setting you choose. Most cameras have two or three settings and resolutions. Resolution is a measurement of how many dots (also called pixels) appear in the picture—the more the better. You may have seen the word megapixel or 1MP on your camera's box when you bought it. This means the top quality setting of the camera takes pictures with a million pixels in them. That's enough to look great when printed out as 5x7s. You'll need 3MP if you want to print out 8x10s.

HELPFUL RESOURCES

CONTACTS	BOOKS
Zap Me's Computer Graphics Tip: zapme.com/net/class/tech/ graphics_tips. html (no www. is needed)	**A Short Course in Choosing & Using a Digital Camera** By Dennis Curtin
	Digital Photography for Dummies By Julie Adair King
	I just bought a Digital Camera, Now What?! by Dave Johnson

e-Finance

6

The whole point of getting a computer is to make your life easier. So start with letting it organize your finances and taxes. How? Read on and find out about various software packages that can help you balance your checkbook and file your taxes. Learn how to use the Internet to shop for a mortgage and keep track of your stocks.

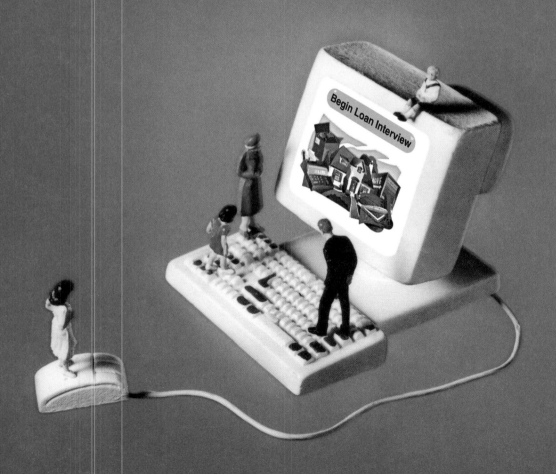

Begin Loan Interview

financial software

Find out where you stand financially with the click of a button

There is nothing wrong with using good ol' paper and pencil to track your finances, but what about next year? You have to start all over again, creating the same categories of income and expenses. What if you decide to update your budget during the year? You do have a budget, don't you? What if your income increases (wouldn't that be nice!) or you switch jobs? If you think it's time to organize your finances—we mean really organize them, not just put the paid bills in a folder in the filing cabinet—you're going to want to consider getting financial software.

Financial software may be just what you need to keep your bills in order and your budget balanced (or, for that matter, create a budget), and make plans for your financial future.

Yes, you do have to enter all the past and future information about your bank accounts and bills into your computer, but it's there for good (or bad—depending on your spending habits). Once you've mastered your financial software, you'll feel it's more than worth the money spent, and that's a good purchase!

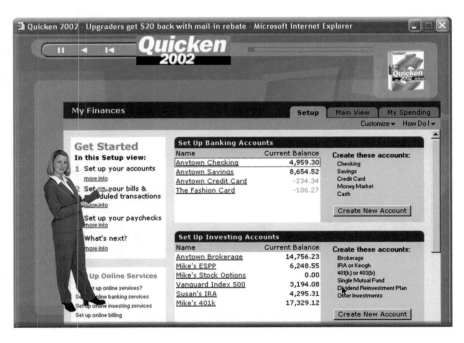

Quicken, a popular financial software, allows you to balance your checkbook, pay bills, and create special lists or graphs for easier viewing of your finances.

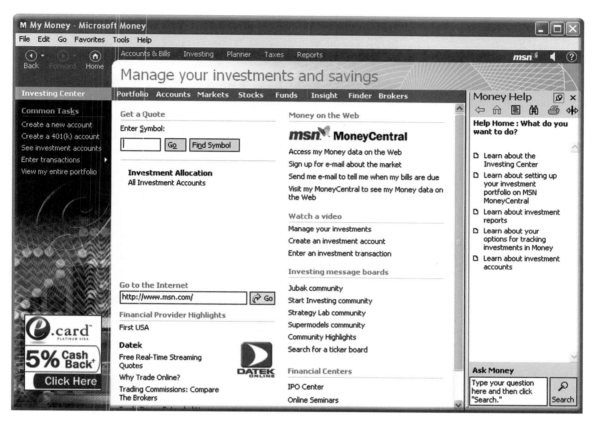

M My Money - Microsoft Money

File Edit Go Favorites Tools Help

Back Forward Home

Accounts & Bills   Investing   Planner   Taxes   Reports

msn

Manage your investments and savings

Investing Center

Portfolio Accounts Markets Stocks Funds Insight Finder Brokers

Common Tasks
Create a new account
Create a 401(k) account
See investment accounts
Enter transactions
View my entire portfolio

Get a Quote

Enter Symbol:

[   ] Go   Find Symbol

Investment Allocation
All Investment Accounts

Go to the Internet
http://www.msn.com/   Go

Financial Provider Highlights
First USA

Datek
Free Real-Time Streaming
Quotes
Why Trade Online?
Trading Commissions: Compare
The Brokers

DATEK
ONLINE

Money on the Web

msn MoneyCentral

Access my Money data on the Web
Sign up for e-mail about the market
Send me e-mail to tell me when my bills are due
Visit my MoneyCentral to see my Money data on
the Web

Watch a video

Manage your investments
Create an investment account
Enter an investment transaction

Investing message boards

Jubak community
Start Investing community
Strategy Lab community
Supermodels community
Community Highlights
Search for a ticker board

Financial Centers

IPO Center
Online Seminars

Money Help

**Help Home : What do you
want to do?**

Learn about the
Investing Center
Learn about setting up
your investment
portfolio on MSN
MoneyCentral
Learn about investment
reports
Learn about your
options for tracking
investments in Money
Learn about investment
accounts

Ask Money

Type your question
here and then click
"Search."

Search

e.card
PLATINUM VISA
5% Cash
Back⁺
Click Here

Microsoft Money, a financial program that is easy to use, includes information on investing, financial planning, and even hints on saving on your taxes.

"MONEY" ON TRIAL

You can visit the Web site www. microsoft.com/money to take a tour of the software and even download a free 90-day trial. (To download software off the Web, see the Internet chapter.) A trial version of software doesn't usually have all the bells and whistles of the purchased package—but it will give you a good idea of how it works.

financial Web sites

All your financial questions can be answered on the Web

The Web now contains such a vast amount of information it's a virtual library in space. To speed your search through it, you need a librarian. In computerland, librarians are called search engines. You might have heard of some of them, Excite or Yahoo! for example. These search engines look through the whole Web for you and bring to your computer screen only what you requested—for example, international mutual funds. However, because financial information is so popular, most search engines have created mini-search engines just for finance and money. Ergo, instead of searching through all of Yahoo! for information on mutual funds, go right to their finance section. How do you do that? Go to your Web address bar and type in **finance.yahoo.com**. (Don't type in www.) Here are some of the financial sections within popular search engines you should check out:

Excite – **quicken.excite.com**
Yahoo! – **finance.yahoo.com**
Microsoft – **moneycentral.msn.com**
Netscape – **personalfinance.netscape.com**

To get to this site directly, type in **finance.yahoo.com** or start at the search engine yahoo.com and follow the channels for financial information.

ASK THE EXPERTS

What sites can give me the latest investment research?

So now that you know how to access search engine channels to learn about your finances, what about investment research? Check out the following site for information on thousands of stocks, mutual funds, and more: **www.morningstar.net**.

What are these calculators that I see on some sites?

Many Web sites include forms that help you determine everything from the size of the mortgage you can afford to the amount of money you need to stash away each year to meet your long-term financial goals. The computer that hosts the Web site calculates the numbers from information you provide and presents an answer tailored to your situation. You can find several useful calculators at **www.kiplinger.com** and **www.bloomberg.com**.

Can Web sites help me figure out foreign currency?

If you're looking at Web sites for an upcoming vacation overseas, you'll want to convert the quoted rates into dollars so you can budget accurately. You need to steer your Web browser to the Universal Currency Converter. When you go there, put the amount to convert in the box at left and then locate the currency you're converting from in the left-hand list. This can be confusing at first, because the site sorts currency alphabetically by country, not the three-digit bank codes that precede each country's name. Once you've found the currency, click on it, then pick USD (U.S. Dollars) in the right-hand column. Click the Perform Currency Conversion button, and you're taken to a page that gives you the exact dollar amount. The converter is located at **www.xe.net/currency/**.

ALL FINANCE, ALL THE TIME

Sometimes, following the market becomes an obsession. When that urge hits, turn to online news sources. Some key locations for round-the-clock coverage:

moneycentral.mscnbc. com
Information as it breaks from one of the leading financial cable channels.

money.cnn.com
Hot stories about business, the economy, and politics from Ted Turner's financial baby.

www.cbsmarketwatch. com
CBS News' site for tracking the day's financial events.

www.thestreet.com
A major source of independent financial news on the Web.

www.fool.com
The Motley Fool provides up-to-date info and down-to-earth advice.

banking online

No more balancing the checkbook each month

The most obvious benefit to online banking is that your checkbook will always be balanced, not to mention no more waiting for your account statement to arrive in the mail, or, for that matter, waiting in line at the bank. You will still get a statement in the mail, but you can review your account online at any time to see recent transactions. To check out online banking services across the country and compare their rates, take a look at this Internet site: **www.cyberinvest.com**. Click on its Banking Center and choose the Guide to Online Banks to see how this brave new world of paperless checks stacks up.

What about security, you ask? Banks take online security very seriously, especially since even the slightest flaw could severely damage customer confidence. For starters, banks have **fire walls** (computer programs that act as gatekeepers so only known customers get in). When banking online, you will have your own passwords and Personal Identification Numbers (PINs). Passwords make sure you are who you claim to be when you log on; PIN codes verify and confirm each banking transaction that you perform. Thanks to

The CyberInvest Web site is the place to go to locate information about online banking services across the country.

encryption (where your data is converted into a series of unrecognizable numbers), none of your personal information (account balances, etc.) can be read by others on the Internet. Encryption creates a series of numbers that acts as a mathematical lock—a lock to which only your financial institution and browser have the key. And every time you create a new transaction, a new lock and key combination is randomly created.

ASK THE EXPERTS

How are monthly fees charged?

Monthly fees are typically deducted automatically from your primary checking account (you designate that on the enrollment form) on the date of your statement.

How do I deposit money into my account?

Your bank should give you postage-paid, addressed envelopes for mailing your deposits directly to the institution. If they don't, ask for some. In addition, you can see if your employer will allow you to set up your paycheck for direct deposit (this is recommended by most financial institutions). Then you can simply verify online that your check was deposited.

How do I get cash?

If only your computer could magically turn into an ATM! Alas, to get money, you need to resort to old-fashioned tactics such as driving to a real bank or an ATM machine. You will be sent an ATM card and PIN number by the good old mail. When you take the money out at a good old-fashioned ATM machine, the withdrawn amount will be immediately posted on your online account.

paying bills online

*Never get
zapped with a
late payment fee
again*

Nothing can make bill paying completely painless. But you can simplify the process with an online bill payment service. This lets you pay anyone with electronic payments, so long as the person or company (called the payee) you owe accepts them. Payments are made either electronically (transferring your money automatically into their account) or by electronic checks. Online tranfers are just like regular checks with the name of your bank and a check number. (They just don't exist on paper.) Great news: You can set up recurring payments for repeat bills such as your rent or mortgage.

Some online companies charge a fee for this service; others provide it free as long as you maintain a minimum balance in your account. Many companies also offer convenient customized reports so you can review your expenses by categories. You can quickly determine, for example, how much you have been paying for groceries for the past six months.

Sounds good, doesn't it? How do you get started? Well, first you can compare the different online banks (check out **www.cyberinvest.com** and **www.bankrate.com** to see various rates). Then simply type in the Web address of the banks you want to check out and review their sites. Are they easy to browse? Do you

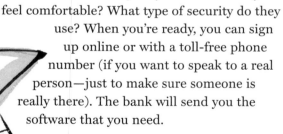

feel comfortable? What type of security do they use? When you're ready, you can sign up online or with a toll-free phone number (if you want to speak to a real person—just to make sure someone is really there). The bank will send you the software that you need.

 # ASK THE EXPERTS

How will paying bills online simplify my life?

Your payments are automatically entered into your online register. You can categorize your payments and print reports for easy management of your finances. Many services even let you export your transactions into your personal financial management software such as Quicken or Microsoft Money.

How long does it take for payees to receive payment?

There are two payment delivery options: electronic and by check. Electronic takes at least three days for your payment to be received and processed and by check takes at least five to seven days for your payment to be received.

How do I know which companies accept online checks?

Call their customer service number and ask. If they do, ask how to sign up. Some companies require written notification that you will be e-mailing payments to them; others let you set up right over the phone.

How can I stop an online check?

If you need to stop payment on an online check, there will be penalties just as if it were a regular paper check. If the online check hasn't been cashed yet, you may be able to cancel it online. Most likely you will have to call the company and explain the problem.

PAYING BILLS BY PHONE

Some companies are still stuck in the 1980s technologically. They're incapable of accepting online payment, but will let you pay bills by phone. Generally, you give them your bank routing number, bank account number, the payment amount, and a specific check number (if it's a checking account). The routing, check, and account numbers are on the bottom left of each of your checks. The bank will deduct the amount directly from your checking account, and it will show up on your next bank statement. The following month (or next time you have a payment), call them with the amount of the bill and a new check number.

shopping for a mortgage

Getting approved (or, yikes, declined) online

The Internet is a great place to research and shop for a home mortgage. Some online mortgage services will also help you calculate how much house you can afford and then help you finance it. To figure out the financing, try these sites:

www.eloan.com—Offers prequalification and preapproval for home-equity loans, first mortgages, and refinancing. Check your loan status online as well as compare the values of neighborhood homes. This site will e-mail you when a particular interest rate becomes available.

www.homeadvisor.msn.com—Features eleven lenders, but has an easy-to-use, 10-step application process and helpful worksheets. It will also suggest ways to meet your home purchasing goals even if you don't qualify for a particular loan.

www.mortgagelocator.com—At this site you type in your rate and terms, and interested lenders contact you. You can also chat online directly with lenders and real estate agents (see "Chatting online," page 76, if you don't know how to do this).

www.quickenloans.quicken.com—You must answer a lot of personal questions to prequalify for a loan. When you finish, a list of possible loans customized for you appears—so you can apply instantly.

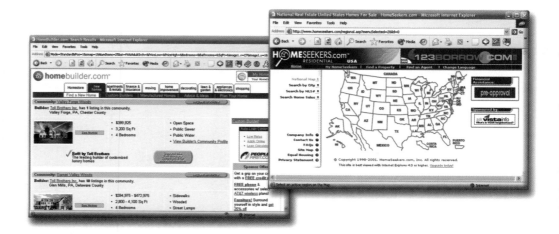

HAT IF

You want to find a house. Can you do this online?

There are a number of online services that will help you find a home in your area. Some will even e-mail you when they find a house that meets your specifications. To get a feel for the home market in your area try:

www.homeadvisor.com—Offers interactive street-level mapping and homes by e-mail, which is a service that saves your search criteria and provides you with an e-mail notification whenever a property meeting your personal housing preference becomes available on the market.

www.realtor.com—Contains over one million homes nationwide contributed by 516 multiple-listing services.

www.homeseekers.com—A daily updated list of over 650,000 homes nationwide.

www.homebuilder.com—A leading home site on the Web with over 125,000 builder listings as well as custom builders.

KEEPING CURRENT

You can check the current interest rate with daily updates on sites like **www.bankrate.com** and **www.banxquote.com**. For purely objective data on interest rates and terms, without all the marketing fluff, check out **www.hsh.com**. It doesn't make loans or accept lender advertising. Instead it surveys 2,500 lenders across the country and updates rates daily.

using tax software

Bet Uncle Sam never dreamed of the e-tax filing

Tax preparation software can save you tons of time filling out tax forms—especially if you decide to take advantage of the online tax filing. Moreover, each new year's software contains the latest tax code changes as well as tax breaks for which you might not have known you qualify. And it will also provide all the forms you will need, so there will be no more running around getting that obscure form before you can file. Best of all, you can even use it to file your federal returns via the Internet.

Two popular tax software programs are Quicken's TurboTax and Kiplinger's TaxCut. Both come with helpful tricks to make filing a breeze. TurboTax has video clips of a real person explaining tax concepts in real English. TaxCut comes with tax tips from the financial experts at *Kiplinger's* magazine.

With the programs, once you have finished entering all the information, you can review for errors, overlooked deductions, and audit alerts. In addition, you can create a customized action plan to help reduce your taxes in the future. When you are ready, you can print your tax return and mail it in, or simply e-mail it.

TurboTax is tax preparation software that includes video clips of a real person explaining tax concepts in plain English so they are easy to understand. If you have trouble hearing the tax lady, your computer's sound level may be too low. Turn up the volume by clicking on your control panel and then selecting sound. You should see a volume control feature you can adjust with your mouse.

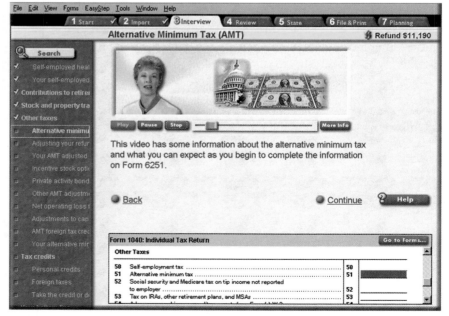

# WHAT IF

You want to download IRS forms?

If you log on to the Internal Revenue Service Web site at **www.irs.ustreas.gov**, you can download IRS forms and follow links to state forms. Choose from either Electronic Services or Forms & Pubs. Note: They are all the way at the bottom of the page—you have to scroll to find them—but they're there.

You want to file your taxes online?

You can use your tax preparation software to file online—the tax preparation software uses an electronic filing center to transmit your encrypted tax data securely over the Internet. Keep in mind that not all states allow electronic filing. Check to see if yours does.

If you've downloaded your IRS forms from the Internet, you can use the IRS Web site at **www.irs.ustreas.gov** to file online after you choose from one of the filing companies they have listed. Don't go with a filing company unless it is IRS-approved. Your online return might not be accepted. Note: The IRS does not post the names of the filing companies until the first of January each year.

You want to find unbiased tax advice?

Visit TaxWeb at **www.irs.com**, which provides links to dozens of Web sites that offer tax-related discussion groups, federal and state tax sites, and tax software developers.

HELP! I NEED SOMEBODY

If you need help understanding something in TurboTax, click the Help button at any time. You can look at frequently asked questions, obtain tax help, review government instructions, read IRS publications, peruse the Money Income Tax Handbook, check out the video library, or go through tax questions and answers.

online investing

Making (or losing) money online

Online brokerage firms basically replace the three-piece suit with your computer, or rather your computer's access to the Internet. In essence, you are making security trades directly online without anyone's advice. By doing this, online brokerage services can lower the fees you pay to buy and sell securities (stocks, bonds, and so on). Many online brokerages still have real-life brokers available to assist you over the phone, but you often pay an additional fee for this service.

Numerous online brokerages actively trade over the Internet. The following are some popular choices: (Note: You do not need www:)

Excite – **quicken.excite.com**

Ameritrade – **ameritrade.com**

Charles Schwab – **schwab.com**

E-Trade – **etrade.com**

Fidelity – **fidelity.com**

Quick and Reilly – **quickandreilly.com**

Online brokerage accounts allow you to buy and sell stocks and bonds directly online without help from a broker. Note the closed padlock at the bottom of the screen that indicates you have a secure connection.

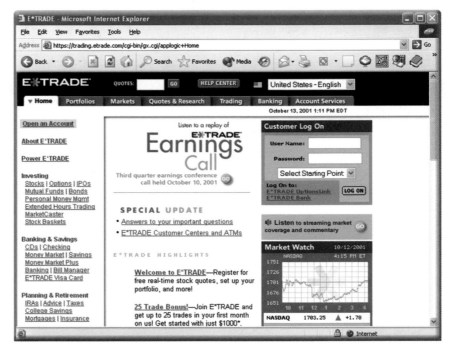

When you set up your online account, you can choose from: individual or joint (you or you and your spouse), professional (businesses), and retirement (IRA) accounts. You will be asked to provide your personal data. Once these are verified, you must sign and return several agreement forms, along with an initial deposit. You will then be given a user ID and password to log on to your online brokerage account. Simply go to your brokerage Web site, type in your password, and start building your portfolio.

ASK THE EXPERTS

What should I look for in an online brokerage?

Find out what services they offer either by calling them on the phone or checking out their Web sites. See what kind of research they have available and whether it will cost you to use it. The fee structure for placing orders should be clearly defined.

What are day traders?

Day traders rapidly buy and sell stocks throughout the day in the hope that their stocks will continue climbing or falling in value for the seconds to minutes they own the stock, allowing them to lock in quick profits. Day traders usually buy on borrowed money, hoping that they will reap higher profits through leverage, but they run the risk of higher losses too.

EDUCATE YOURSELF

The Securities and Exchange Commission (SEC) has several Web pages devoted to the Internet and on-line trading at **www.sec.gov**. Click on the Investor Education link and review information from the Investor Education and Assistance office.

FIRST PERSON DISASTER

Online Trading Addiction

I feel like I could go on Oprah or something: *The Mom Who Became A Day Trader Junkie.* It started out innocently enough. All I wanted to do was be able to keep a better eye on my stocks so I signed up with an e-trade outfit that gives you instant updates on the stock market. It was so easy to get an e-account, and after one week I made my first trade online. I felt very hip. Now all I feel is exhausted. The problem is that it's so easy to check your stocks any time of day or night, that any sudden market move can drive you nuts. Guess what? Sometimes the market shifts every five minutes. There were days when I never left the house. All I did was watch my e-trade account. It got so bad that I missed my daughter's tennis tournament. She came home sobbing because I wasn't there. I knew then and there it was time to call it quits. I transferred my whole e-account to a broker. Let him worry about it for me.

Mimi K., Morristown, New Jersey

now what do I do?

Answers to common problems

My tax preparation software isn't showing any of its video features.

Each time you use the program, put the original CD-ROM disk in the CD-ROM drive. In order for its interactive features to work, some software packages require the CD-ROM to be in place.

What is www.priceline.com and how do I use it?

It's an online service that lets you bid for many goods and services, including airfares and automobiles. You can also bid for a home mortgage, equity loan, or refinancing. Simply complete the online loan request with the rate and terms you desire, and you will be notified via e-mail within six business hours by one of four participating lenders. If your exact rate and terms are accepted—the lender requires a $200 good-faith deposit when they make an offer—the sum is credited toward closing costs. (For more information, see auctions, page 74.)

How can I increase my Web browser security?

Make sure you use a browser with the best and latest encryption techniques—this usually means the latest version of the browser software. Also, utilize the built-in security features of your **browser** (the software that lets you access the Internet). Open your browser and look for the menu bar at the top. Click on View. In Microsoft's Internet Explorer, click on Internet Options. A box will appear with a row of tabbed little pages on it. Click on the Security tab. It will walk you through any changes you would like to make to upgrade your security.

Can hackers eavesdrop on my visits to an online bank?

Hackers can't break into a secure connection between your PC and a Web site. So how do you know whether your connection's secure? There are two ways: The Web address of a site during a normal connection begins with http://. If you're on a secure site, the Web address starts with https://. The "s" stands for secure. If you look at the bottom of your Web browser screen, you'll also see a little padlock icon. If it's a closed padlock, the connection's secure. (See the picture on p. 126.) If it's open, it's not secure, but the chances are slim either way that someone's snooping on you.

Where can I find out more about filing taxes electronically?

There are three ways to "e-file," as the government geeks like to call it. These options include having a tax professional file for you, filing yourself through a personal computer, or filing over the telephone. Just visit **www.irs.ustreas.gov**, click on Electronic Services, then click on IRS e-file for Individuals.

Why can't my computer read the documents I downloaded from the IRS site?

The government puts its tax forms and documents in a special format called PDF (portable document format). These print out almost exactly like the forms you get from tax offices on pretty much all computer printers—but they need a special program called Adobe Acrobat Reader to view and print the files. If your computer doesn't already have Adobe Acrobat Reader installed, visit http://**www.adobe.com/products/acrobat/readermain.html** to download it for free.

Can I keep the information I've entered in Microsoft Money safe?

You can keep your files safe in two ways—safe from prying eyes, and also safe from being accidentally deleted. To protect your files with a password so that only people typing in the password can open the file, select the File menu and click on Log in Lockbox. You can use this option to change a password too, in case you suspect someone's guessed it. To keep your information safe from being deleted, make a backup. Select the File menu and click on Back Up.

Can Quicken make sure I won't miss any bill payment dates?

Sure! Just check an old bill for the time of the month it's usually due. Then open Quicken and point to the Bills icon. Choose Schedule a Future Payment and find the bill type from the list to the right of the calendar. Move your mouse pointer over to the bill type and drag it to a date. Fill in the details and click on OK. You're set! Now repeat this process for ALL your bills.

ELPFUL RESOURCES

CONTACTS	BOOKS
Quicken support intuit.com/support/quicken/	**Banking Online for Dummies** By Dan Gookin
Microsoft Money support support.microsoft.com	
TurboTax intuit.com/support/turbotax/	
TaxCut support www.taxcut.com	

e-Genealogy

7

Getting back to your roots was never so easy as with a computer. In this chapter you'll learn how to use the Internet and the various software packages out there to research your family history and pull it together into a real family tree. It's as easy as pie—make that grandma's apple pie.

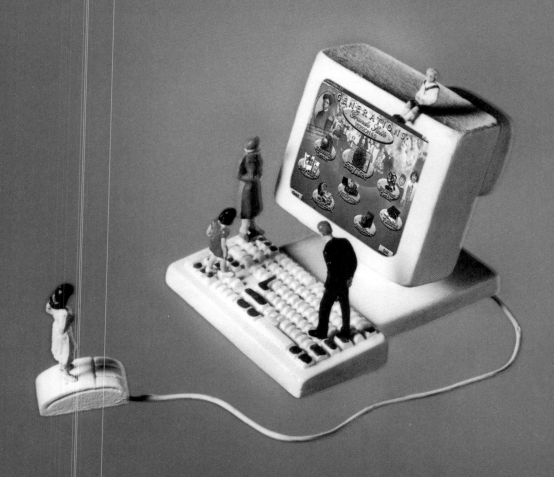

genealogy Web sites

Finding out where you came from can be a fun adventure on the Web

You bought your computer to be a part of the cutting- edge future, but you can also use it to shine a light into your past. The Web is filled with many sites dedicated to genealogy and creating a family tree. Whether you want to keep track of your immediate family—like brothers and sisters, aunts and uncles—or you want to reach back several generations to discover if you are related to the British royal family, the Web can help.

There's plenty of good news: The Web is chock full of sites dedicated to family lineage research, and many of them are free. The most important elements of these sites are the databases, which are records of information. A database can be something as simple as a telephone directory or it can be as specialized as Maryland Revolutionary War records or a list of births in Montgomery County, Virginia, from 1653 to 1812. Some are arranged by date, such as census records for 1890, others by location—say, the Civil War veterans from Cayuga County, New York.

For an online genealogy search, consult the following Web sites:

www.ancestry.com   **www.familysearch.com**
www.cyndislist.com   **www.genealogy.com**

The welcome page or home page of Ancestry.com shows you where to go to create a family tree and how to start a search for an ancestor.

ASK THE EXPERTS

What's the best way to get started?

Look at a number of genealogical sites to see what they offer. Browse through them to see not only their particular features but also how comfortable you are navigating around. Look at the types of databases they offer—are Civil War veterans or census records from 1890 relevant to you? Be sure to use whichever features are free to get an idea of the scope of the site.

Can I get information about my family for free?

There are plenty of free Web sites dedicated to managing your present clan. For most of these sites you can build a family tree and create a family Web site for no charge. However, if you want to conduct an online search, you'll either have to subscribe to the particular Web site or pay for the specific search. Sites will ask you to type in your credit card number. Also, many of the sites include advertising that is frankly hard to ignore for various products such as software and books. Although it's not necessary to purchase anything, the advertising makes it seem as though it is.

LOOK BEFORE YOU LEAP

Some genealogy Web sites charge a fee. Before you commit to a genealogy Web site and subscribe, make sure to look around the site as much as possible. Before paying money, check out the Web site's features, free tools (like the family tree builder and family Web site center), and the description of records you can then access.

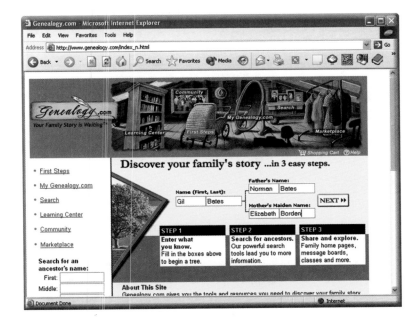

The welcome page of Genealogy.com leads you to a variety of activities related to building a family tree and researching ancestors.

genealogy online

Use the Web to research your family history

How do these genealogy Web sites work? In most cases the **welcome** or **splash** screen (this is a Web site's home or main page) has a few empty boxes where you fill in your name, date of birth, and the name of the ancestor you're looking for. Registration is usually free. Most sites offer a variety of genealogical features that are fun to play with. Here's a sampling:

www.ancestry.com—This is a good program if you have modest lineage goals. It offers a chance to view a **message board,** a place on its site where you can post messages to other people with the same family name. You can leave a message like, "I'm searching for the Dover family of Albany, New York. I believe they moved there in the 1890s and most of the family stayed in the upstate New York area."

www.familysearch.com—Get ready. This site lets you consult a higher power! It is the Internet Genealogy Service for the Church of Jesus Christ of Latter-day Saints. The Mormon Church is world famous for its records and research into family lineage. The browse categories at this site are extensive. You can also create a free starter family tree once you register.

FamilySearch.com, the genealogical service of the Mormon Church, allows you to search for information about ancestors in a variety of records: census reports, property records, voting registers, veterans groups, and more.

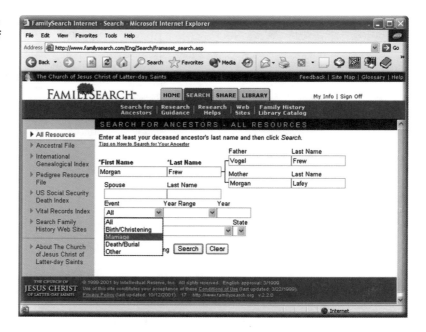

Note: You will be asked to create and submit a GEDCOM file, which is a standard family tree file, but it's not required. If you do create a GEDCOM file, you can submit it to the Church of Jesus Christ of Latter-day Saints (or LDS) for its records. Then your file will be in the vast archives in the Granite Mountain Records Vault near Salt Lake City, Utah.

www.genealogy.com—This is another friendly site, but it includes advertising for its genealogy software. There's a link on the welcome page for people that answers basic questions about creating a family tree. It also has Web links to other pages within Genealogy.com to help you get started.

www.cyndislist.com—It's a vast collection of links (more than 109,700!) to other genealogy sites on the Web. It is strong, if a bit confusing, with links to adoption records, famous people, foreign records, heraldry, and much more. And if you've hit a wall in your research, this site offers a link to professional genealogy veterans and experts. Some offer free advice; others charge a fee.

FIRST PERSON DISASTER

Software Gone Soft

I gave my husband this incredible genealogy software package for his birthday. He could not wait to try it. He put it in the CD-ROM drive and waited for the software picture to appear on our computer desktop. All he got was an obscure error message. He tried loading it again. Same error message. I could feel my blood pressure rising. The computer was only a few months old and already it was broken. Then I had the bright idea to call the software maker and find out what was wrong. I found the number on the back of the box and called. After a few minutes on hold I got a real person and told him our problem. "Oh, yeah, there was a problem with one of the batches of CDs that went out. Sorry. If you give me your address I'll mail you a replacement." I was so relieved there wasn't something seriously wrong with our computer that I wasn't even mad at their sloppy quality control.

Roberta T., San Diego, California

genealogy software

For a sharper family search, try genealogy software

Sure, the Web is a great place to mosey around to find your past, but there's plenty of software that offers more information, tools, and features than these genealogy Web sites. And once you've paid for the software, which usually ranges in price from $50 to $80, you have access to the hundreds of thousands of names that come with the program.

How do these programs manage to deliver all of this information? Simple. Along with the software, you get several CD-ROMs (disks with information on them). You load these CDs one by one into your CD-ROM drive (see pages 24–25). Some genealogy software comes with lots of CDs. Do yourself a favor and buy a CD-ROM rack for your software shelf for easy access.

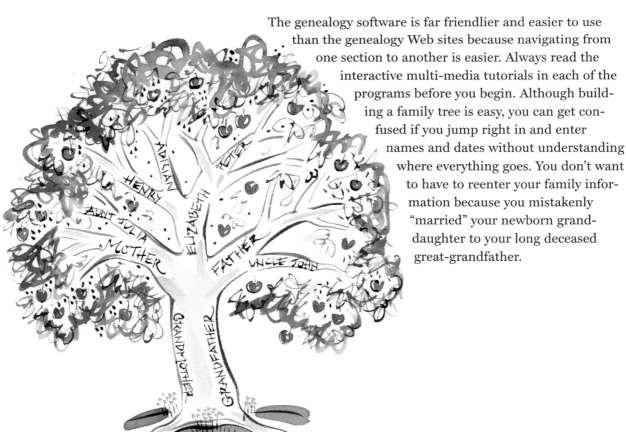

The genealogy software is far friendlier and easier to use than the genealogy Web sites because navigating from one section to another is easier. Always read the interactive multi-media tutorials in each of the programs before you begin. Although building a family tree is easy, you can get confused if you jump right in and enter names and dates without understanding where everything goes. You don't want to have to reenter your family information because you mistakenly "married" your newborn granddaughter to your long deceased great-grandfather.

The splash page from Generations Grand Suite software offers you a number of icons to click on to get started.

Generations

Generations is a complete family research solution. This program from SierraHome (**www.sierra.com**) blends research with a down-home memory keeper. Not only can you store family recipes in MasterCook and family photos in SnapShot Express, this family tree behemoth comes with 21 CD-ROMs with more than 300,000 names and resources.

more software

In Family Tree Maker, another software package, you can locate ancestors and establish your family tree.

Family Tree Maker

This program from Broderbund software (**www.broderbund.com**) comes packed with a staggering number of CD-ROMs with an index of 250 million names, the Social Security Death Index, birth records of the U.S. and Europe from 900 to 1880, passenger lists for the people who arrived in the U.S. early last century, and more. In this exhaustive collection you can also create genealogy reports, family trees with photographs, world maps, time lines, ancestor trees, and family group sheets. And you can create multimedia scrapbooks with scanned documents, photos, and sketches, as well as video and sound clips. If the rest of your family is online, you can publish your family research as a Web page for your extended family to view.

This program is straightforward if not terribly pleasing to the eye. It's by far the easiest to enter and add information to. The simplified icons on the tool bar clearly illustrate what they deliver.

Copyright ©1999 Individual Software Inc. This software is for the use by a single user only. It is not licensed for use on any type of network. The software is protected under Federal Copyright Law. It is illegal to make or distribute copies of this software.

Family Ties family chart is easy to fill out. If you make a mistake, simply delete the name and type in a new one.

Family Ties Deluxe Edition

This program, available from Individual Software (**www.individualsoftware.com/new/consumerdetails/ft_details.htm**) uses the Web to perform searches for family history. With a click of an icon the software launches your Web browser and sends you to **Ancestry.com** and **FamilySearch.com** for more information.

So if the software goes out to the Web, why buy the program? Because it contains genealogy projects like creating attractive family trees, pedigree reports, and tools for creating your own family tree Web page. Some of the CD-ROMs in this set of four include Progeny's Social Security Death Index—information on 61 million people born in the 19th and 20th centuries; the Francis Firth Collection—an archive of photographs dating from 1860 to 1970; and the Centennial Working Model Edition—a historical time line of people, places, and events, with animated maps of Europe and the Middle East.

Family Ties Deluxe Edition is a basic genealogy program; it won't win any beauty pageants, but it's easy to use. You can create a family tree within minutes.

building a family tree

Creating a heart-warming visual expression of your family's history

Celebrate your family's history—even if it's full of quirks and oddball relatives—by making a family tree. The final step is pretty much the same regardless of the software package you use. After you've typed in all of the family names you've found and your tree is "complete," go to the menu bar and and click on Tree or Easy/Tree and see how it automatically makes a tree for you. On the next page, find step-by-step instructions using the Generations software.

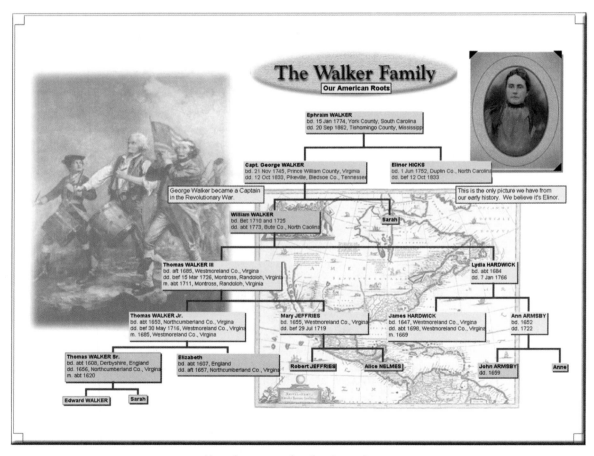

How do you get family photos into your tree? You need to scan them in. (See pages 106–107 to learn how to do that.)

STEP BY STEP: BUILDING A TREE

1. Load the software CD-ROM disks into your computer. (See page 24 for information on how to do that.)

2. After you've loaded the software, click the EasyTree icon in the "splash" or welcome screen, which displays all of the elements of the software program.

3. A blank index card will appear with boxes to fill in. Type in information requested, such as your name, date of birth, occupation, education, religion, and any notes.

4. Next to each index card is a tiny icon of a Plus Sign. Click the Plus Sign once, and a small drop-down menu appears for adding new family members. Add your spouse's information.

5. Then begin entering information about your children or your parents. When that's done, add your siblings and their spouses and children. Keep going until you've done all you can.

6. If you've scanned photographs of family members into your PC or taken pictures with a digital camera, you can add images. Click on Window from the drop-down menu and select Images. An Image dialogue box will appear. Click the Add Image button and find the image stored on your hard disk.

7. Sort through your family tree for different views. Click the Overview button (marked "o'view") to view a breakdown of your tree by family members. Click on the name of the family member for a new view.

8. Time to make a chart. Click File from the drop-down menu and select EasyChart, which will automatically launch that portion of Generations Grand Suite. Browse through the drop-down menus in EasyChart to select different chart views, from TimeLine, Pedigree, Descendant, and Enhanced Hourglass.

9. Don't worry about saving your family tree; these programs have an AutoSave feature that automatically saves the file.

now what do I do?

Answers to common problems

What can I add to spice up my family tree to make it look nice?

With your new computer, you can create attractive family trees with as much information as you like. If you have a **scanner** (a device that copies material on paper into a digital document or piece of art (see pages 106–107), you can include photos of relatives or even a scanned image of your wedding invitation. For the "family reports" feature that's found on some programs, you can add video clips, sound and music clips, as well as specific records like military discharge papers or medical records.

I don't have a scanner. How can I get my photos inserted?

Try contacting a local copy shop or graphics shop. They have scanners and computers and for a fee will scan in your photos and give them to you on a computer disk that you can then load onto your computer at home. They can also edit your photos (get out all those red eyes from the flashbulb). They can also "stitch" together ripped photographs.

How long should I expect to take creating my family tree?

It depends entirely on how much detail you want. If you're creating a three-generation family tree (grandparents/children/grandchildren), you can accomplish this in an afternoon. But if you're venturing back centuries and to other continents, then it could be a long search.

Should I worry about entering my family's names into a strange Web site?

Look for genealogy Web sites (and all Web sites for that matter) that offer a Privacy Statement, passwords, and a promise not to sell your data to marketing companies.

What are newsgroups?

These are Internet groups dedicated to a specific topic; they have their own message boards where people can leave questions, notes—whatever they feel is germane to the topic. There are many genealogical newsgroups based on ethnic groups, geographical locations, religious affiliations, and even surnames. The information here is not necessarily from official databases, but rather from individual people's experiences in doing research. Newsgroups provide an additional source for information, as well as opinions and guidance.

What is shareware?

Shareware is computer software that you pay for on the honor system. Shareware programs usually have a 30-day free trial period. If you like it, you should support it with your cash. After that, the programs will show reminder screens asking you to license the software (i.e., pay up). There are a number of genealogy shareware programs out there. (To download them from the Web, see page 80.)

Can I e-mail the family tree to my relatives?

Sure you can. Just attach it to an e-mail message as you would any other file. (See pages 92-93 for more info on attaching e-mail.) Or if you are feeling really brave, you can create a Web page with the information along with an Internet Family Book with Family Tree Maker, complete with information and multimedia files. With a Web page, any family member with a computer and an Internet account can view your work. And there's a wonderful side benefit to posting your family tree online: Other long-lost family members or branches of the family tree can find your family tree and contact you. That way your family tree can become broader and deeper.

How can other relatives contribute to the family tree?

Let them e-mail memories, anecdotes, pictures, even video clips to the Web page. Plan a family reunion so everyone can contribute to the family lore!

 ELPFUL RESOURCES

CONTACTS	BOOKS
Generations Grand Suite www.sierra.com	**Family Tree Maker for Dummies** By Matthew L. Helm and April Leigh Helm
Family Tree Maker www.broderbund.com	
Family Ties www.individualsoftware.com	**Genealogy Online for Dummies** By Matthew L. Helm

e-Travel

8

He won't ask for directions;
she won't look at a map. Thanks to the computer,
this age-old dilemma has been solved.
In this chapter you'll see how simple it is to go
online and get instant directions as well as tips on
using trip-planning software packages.

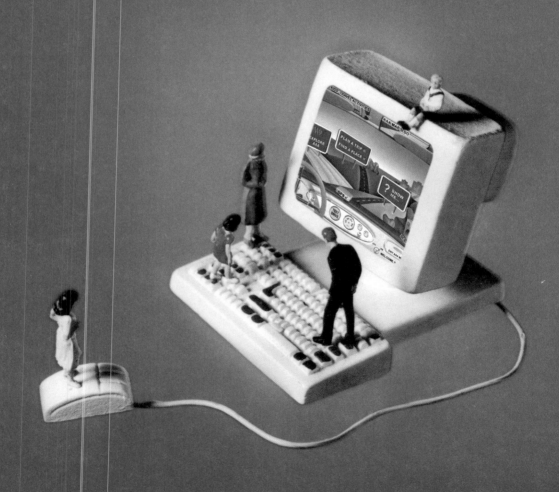

planning a trip

You'll never have to fold a map again

Use your PC the next time you venture out of your home? Not exactly. Only **laptop** owners (who have a portable computers with built-in batteries) can actually take them on the road. That said, you can use your PC, the Web, and some special software for planning your next trip.

Family trips no longer mean large maps that never fold back into their original shape. With Web maps and trip-planning software, you can print out explicit directions from your home to Aunt Sally's farm. And unlike those old maps that make you do your own plotting, you can print out maps with the details you need. For example, you'll find maps that point out landmarks that tell you where to make a left turn or if you've gone too far.

Also, with a click of the mouse you can find the shortest route to save on gas or, if you have the time, get directions for the scenic route. Need a place to stay? Click the lodging icon and you'll find a list of accommodations ranging from four-star hotels to budget motels. Want a bite to eat? Click the food icon, and a list of restaurants appears, with everything from filet mignon to Big Macs. Theater, the local hospital, shopping districts? All that and more are a click away with most trip-planning Web sites and software.

Old maps are fine to keep in an emergency, but thanks to computer printouts you can now have exact directions.

**A LITTLE PRACTICE
GOES A LONG WAY**

Practice makes perfect. Before you use a Web site or software, try making a set of travel directions to someplace you already know. To familiarize yourself with the step-by-step procedure, print out directions to your cousin's house or to your family's favorite vacation spot.

ASK THE EXPERTS

What makes maps from software and the Web so special?

Think of them as smart maps. Instead of poring over paper trying to figure out how to get from point A to point B, your computer maps out the shortest, fastest, most scenic, and up-to-date route for you.

What is GPS?

It stands for Global Positioning System. This system was developed by the military to help people pinpoint exactly where they are, all over the world. It has two parts: satellites in orbit sending radio signals that cover the earth, and a GPS receiver that uses the signals to calculate exactly where you are. You can buy handheld GPS receivers or ones that plug into your laptop computer that will put a big You are Here arrow in your map software. Some top-of-the-line automobiles already have GPS and mapping software built in (and Hertz rental cars come with an optional NeverLost GPS system.) GPS should become a standard feature in new cars over the next few years.

using the Web to plan a trip

Let the Web sites tell you exactly where to go

Terrific customized directions for your next business or family trip are as close as your Web browser, and they're free (although they do come with the advertising that pays the bills for the Web site).

So how do trip-planning Web sites work? All are simple to use. You go to the Web site and

- type in your street address, city, state, and zip code
- then type in the same information for your destination
- click the Calculate button

After a few seconds, depending on the speed of your modem (the device that connects your computer to the Internet), a detailed map will appear with directions. Some of these sites also offer directions for getting home.

Along with travel maps, there are links to other Web sites for practically all of your travel needs: hotels and motels, car rental, events in the local area, and more. But be aware that a free mapping Web site is often a front door to online travel merchants, so the information may not be impartial or complete. Often, Web sites have specific partnerships with car rental companies, hotel chains, and restaurants.

For planning a trip, consult the following Web sites:

> **www.mapblast.com**
>
> **www.mapquest.com**
>
> **www.expediamaps.com**

MapBlast

MapBlast (**www.mapblast.com**) gives step-by-step directions, even for major roads and highways, and an estimated length of time a trip should take (these are extremely optimistic—it's best to add time for traffic, construction, and rest and refueling breaks). You can also get step-by-step maps, a map of how to get home, and with a nifty hot-air balloon icon, you can zoom in on your map.

You can e-mail the map and directions to friends and family for parties or family reunions. When you print, you get a choice of full color, grayscale, and black and white. There are links to other services: to find a nearby Hilton hotel, to the Barnes & Noble Web site to find travel books, and to Web sites for ski vacations, bed-and-breakfasts, car rentals, scheduled events, and live traffic reports.

MOVING TO A NEW HOUSE

You've recently moved into a new house and want to give all your friends and family directions without having to repeat "Turn left at the gas station and drive for about 3/10ths of a mile . . ." every time someone calls. Create a map to your house from a central point—the exit ramp of the Interstate or the town square—and include it in the change-of-address cards that you send out.

more Web sites

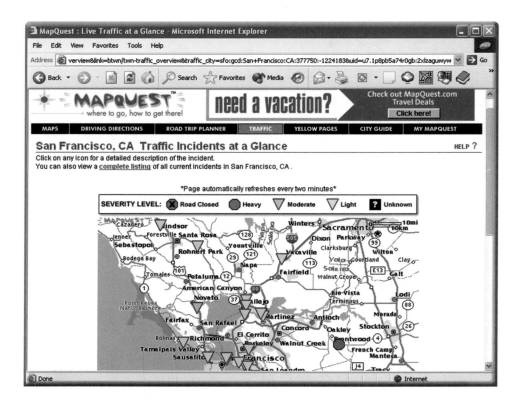

MapQuest

MapQuest (**www.mapquest.com**) has a lot to offer anyone planning a trip (although it's not as easy to use as MapBlast). Not only can you find directions for your next trip, there's a section for live traffic reports for more than 35 U.S. cities: perfect for people who bring their laptops on the road with them. There's also mapping based on area codes and telephone exchanges in the U.S., and postal-code mapping for Great Britain. The Travel Guide has information about lodging, food, city info, and weather reports that help you decide whether or not to bring a jacket. If you're interested in a GPS system for your laptop and car, MapQuest has a link to the EarthMate GPS Receiver.

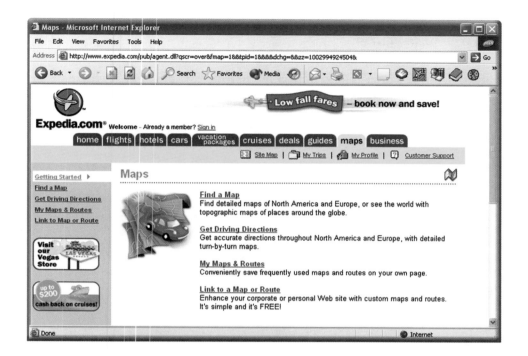

ExpediaMaps

ExpediaMaps (**www.expediamaps.com**) from Microsoft, the software giant, is a Web site with maps for free. In order to take advantage of the site, you have to register your name and provide an e-mail address. It's free and only takes a minute. One thing to note: When you enter your name, you cannot have any spaces, so use an underscore (press the Shift key and then the Hyphen key above the letter P on your keyboard. Example: Jane_Smith). When choosing your map, you can select among Shortest, Quickest, and Scenic. ExpediaMaps has a few quirks: You have to enter in abbreviations for streets, roads, and drives for best results, such as "Main St." instead of the complete "Main Street." Although ExpediaMaps offers much of the same information as MapQuest and MapBlast, ExpediaMaps is really an online advertisement for the retail software version, Microsoft Expedia Streets & Trips.

CRYING OUT FOR COLOR

Of course, you can print out maps for your family vacation or business trip that are accurate and easy to read on a black-and-white printer. But for a party invitation or family reunion, a map just begs for color. Even a low-end color printer will produce gorgeous and useful maps. (To save your color ink, you can print vacation maps in black and white or grayscale on your color printer.)

creating maps

Getting personalized directions

Every Web site has its own style of map. On some the lettering of the streets is larger, on some the streets are wider, on some the landmarks are more clearly designated. To see which style works best for you, follow the step-by-step directions below for comparing the same map on three Web sites.

When you have decided which map you find easiest to read, then go to the links on that site to get the additional information you need to complete your trip.

STEP BY STEP: COMPARING MAPS

How do you know which online map-planning Web site to use? Simple. Give each one a road test by comparing what routes they select to get to the same destination.

1. Type in the name of the first Web site.

2. Enter in your address and the address of your destination.

3. Print out the map they give.

4. Do the same at other map sites.

5. Compare the maps.

Using these steps, we decided to plot a road trip from Long Island, New York, to Washington, DC. Although the three Web sites gave the same directions, more or less (opposite page), the maps differed on the local road directions and in the estimated time it would take to get there.

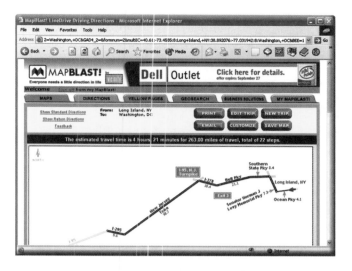

www.MapBlast.com

MapBlast gave four different options for printing a map: full-color, grayscale, black-and-white, or text directions. Once you choose the color scheme, MapBlast doesn't offer a print preview to see how your map will print out. The directions were legible and offered directions with 24 steps. MapBlast estimated that the trip was 245 miles and would take 3 hours, 55 minutes. And you can save the map to your computer too.

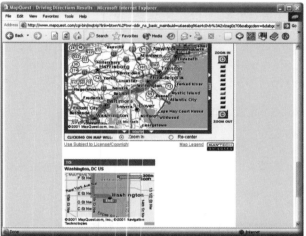

www.MapQuest.com

MapQuest has far superior printing options. At first we had a useful map that was crowded with a ton of banner ads and Web links, but after clicking the 'Printer Friendly Version' button, all but two of the banner ads disappeared. The map printed out two pages with 25 steps, although the bottom direction of the first page and the top direction of the second page didn't print clearly. MapQuest estimated the trip to be 251.2 miles long and would take 4 hours, 53 minutes—one hour longer than MapBlast.

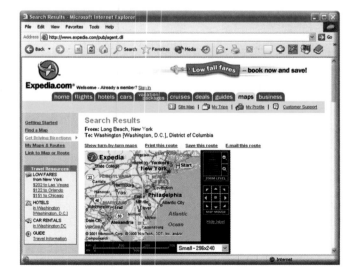

www.Expediamaps.com

Talk about information! After entering the starting and destination addresses, Microsoft's ExpediaMaps offered a six-page map with 130 steps for our directions—56 from Long Island, New York, to the New Jersey border alone. And although we selected the shortest route, ExpediaMaps estimated that our trip would take 6 hours, 56 minutes—that's two hours more than MapQuest! And not only can you save the map, the Web site offers turn-by-turn maps, navigable maps, and an e-mail option for sending the map to friends or family members.

trip-planning software

Become your own travel consultant thanks to these special features

Love maps? Then be prepared to be dazzled with mapping software. Think of these computer maps as maps that have magically come to life. They not only give you the same information as a trusty old paper map but they also plot out directions, help you create a detailed itinerary, let you choose between the quickest and most scenic routes, and show you points of interest along the route. Like the Web sites, they also give you plenty of information about hotels, restaurants, and campgrounds. The programs are easy to use. First load the software (see page 24). Then enter your starting place or home address and your destination, and the program creates a map. Here are a few popular trip-planning software packages:

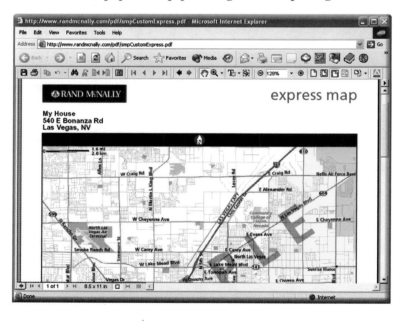

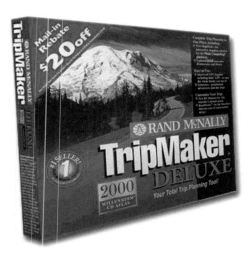

Rand McNally TripMaker Deluxe Edition

Remember Rand McNally maps in grade school? Now it's time to graduate to Rand McNally's TripMaker Deluxe Edition software. Like other programs, you enter your home address and your destination and Rand McNally does the rest. You can download the maps to your electronic handheld organizer so you can bring the maps with you. You can check out the RV Planner for the special parks and services if you're traveling with the family camper. And if you have a GPS device, the software comes with the Kid's GPS Planet Earth Navigator for the younger travelers. For more information check out **www.randmcnally.com** before you purchase.

Microsoft Expedia Streets & Trips

Microsoft ExpediaMaps has an interesting approach: It uses as few buttons as possible, so it resembles Internet Explorer, Microsoft's Web browser. Even with this stripped-down approach, this program has road information, address-to-address maps, and a Snap Routing feature that lets you add a new route to your travel itinerary. Extras include lists of more than 25,000 hotels, 300,000 InfoUSA business listings, 14,000 *Zagat Survey* restaurant surveys, and links to 10,000 Web sites for road construction or weather updates. You can strip unneeded information from the map or print different kinds of maps. And you can check out the software at **www.microsoft.com/expedia** before buying.

BUY OR BROWSE

So why purchase mapping software when you can browse maps on the Web? The software has more information and special features: You can print out maps and itineraries with only the information you need and no annoying ads. Most programs have extensive Web links for finding hotel rates, traffic reports, restaurant updates, and more. In all, the trip-planning software offers the best of both worlds: software and Web sites.

more trip software

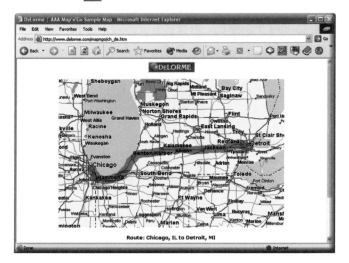

Create a map that finally puts the backseat driver to shame.

DeLorme's AAA Map 'n' Go

DeLorme's AAA Map 'n' Go does everything but take the wheel for a few hours. Based on the AAA maps we grew up with, this program has detailed maps and travel advice as well as AAA TourBook listings with ratings of more than 66,000 AAA-approved restaurants, hotels, campgrounds, and diversions. Along with GPS Voice Navigation support for your laptop, the GPS receiver (sold separately) can read the directions to you as you drive. Finally, a backseat driver that actually helps make the trip easier.

Along with planning either the quickest or most scenic route, AAA Map 'n' Go will calculate the cost of your trip, factoring in gas and tolls. And with the Via routing tool, you can add alternate routes, such as using mountain roads or skirting outside inner-city traffic. And laptop computer users can download maps for light and easy map consulting. Check out the company Web site before buying at **delorme.com**.

WHAT IF

You need more information for your trip?

Before you pack, consult your trip software for answers to a variety of important travel issues.

You want to know if Fido can go along?

If the thought of leaving your pet in a kennel makes you break out in hives, then check out the pet traveling tips in these titles. With a few mouse clicks you can find out what hotels and motels allow pets.

You want to see America on $30 a day?

Use the budget planners to make sure you stay within the amount of money you have allotted. In DeLorme's AAA Map 'n' Go, for example, you can set your Budget Planner with several different categories, such as accommodations, admission fees, dining, gas, gifts, laundry, shopping, and tolls.

You need an answer to the cry "We're huuuungry!"

All the programs help you find different styles of cuisine on your trip. Feel like Chinese food in North Carolina or a Mexican meal in Ohio? Just enter your preferences into the mapping software, the radius you're willing to drive for food—say, 10 miles—and you'll find directions to what will be your new favorite eating establishments. Bon appetit!

You want to stretch those legs?

Driving nonstop is for truck drivers and college students on the way to spring break. To ensure a safe arrival and to avoid driving monotony, make sure to schedule breaks from driving. Trip-planning software programs list all of the rest stops, historical points of interest, and parks on your trip.

GETTING THERE FROM HERE

Map software is very accurate. Delorme's AAA Map 'n' Go software, for example, uses the same maps as the AAA. And maps provided in the Rand McNally software come from—you guessed it— Rand McNally. They are very reliable.

online travel agent

Book a flight, rental car, and hotel room from your Web browser

The Web can put you in control of planning a trip. Online trip-planning services present you with numerous flights to a location, tell you of multiple hotels near your final destination, and give a full list of car rental companies at your destination airport (or downtown if you prefer). And these sites are open for business whenever wanderlust strikes.

Want to see how much it would cost to stop off and see Aunt Edna in Chicago? Try out as many options as you like. If prices look too high now, you can save the itinerary and come back in a few weeks when the airlines are having a price war.

Heads up: Each of these sites requires that you register before accessing information. They also request credit card information that will be used to bill tickets and make reservations. But the benefits are enormous, even if you are just an armchair traveler.

Some popular e-travel sites:
www.expedia.com—Doing research on a possible trip? Visit Microsoft's travel Web site and check out dates for different departures and returns. The site saves several itineraries, so you can consult with spouse, family, or friends before committing to a particular trip.

www.travelocity.com—Helps you find a plane trip to match your most important criteria. Willing to trade an extra stop for a lower fare? Just tell it that price is more important than a nonstop flight.

www.biztravel.com—Business travel is different from personal travel. For one thing, schedule convenience outweighs price in most situations. Among other benefits of **biztravel.com**, you can keep track of the frequent flier mileage for multiple airlines.

www.priceline.com—Finally, you get some control over flight costs and hotel room rates. Priceline lets you set a price you'd pay, and companies tell you whether they're willing to meet your price. It's a great way to get a last-second ticket on the cheap for a weekend visit to a major U.S. city.

ASK THE EXPERTS

Does it matter which site I use?

Personal preference will ultimately decide which location you select to make travel reservations. Each interface has its quirks, but these Web sites all tend to tap into common databases of flight information.

Why can't I find bigger discounts?

Some budget airlines and hotels don't show up in online travel agency databases. You may have to go directly to the budget company's Web sites or poke around for online bargains at such sites as **www.cheaptickets.com**.

FREQUENT BROWSER

Wondering whether you've accrued enough miles to take a free trip? Most airlines let you access information about your frequent flier program online. You can also update such information as your mailing address and book flights with your miles, without the hassle of listening to an annoyed operator on the other end of the phone line as you ask to try different options.

Trying to keep next summer's vacation affordable? Travel sites like Travelocity help you plan in advance and search for an indirect flight to cut costs.

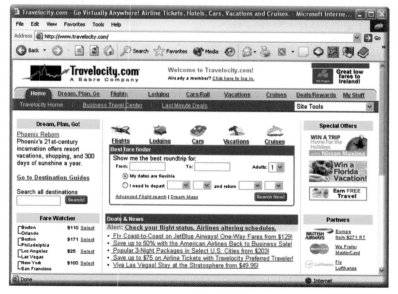

159

city guides

Find out what's going on in the towns you'll be visiting

Few things are as bad as arriving in a distant city full of excitement and not knowing what to do—except possibly returning someplace you used to live only to learn that all your old haunts are gone. Thanks to city guides on the Web, you can find out what movie, concert, or museum exhibit is currently showing in almost every town in the country.

Not surprisingly, major cities have some of the most extensive coverage. The two best locations for getting the scoop on big cities are the CitySearch and DigitalCities services (a lot of detail, but only major cities) and Yahoo's Metro guides (less data, but more cities). Each of these sites can link you to a screening of the latest Hollywood epic and a good place for a quick bite to eat afterward.

For the larger cities, several sites compete with Yahoo, CitySearch, and DigitalCities to provide information. One good source is generally the local newspaper, which often has its own area guide such as *The New York Times'* **www.nytoday.com/pages/nytoday/**. The Web sites of alternative newspapers, such as the *San Francisco Bay Guardian*, are another source of what's going on in big towns.

City guides steer you to the happenings in your hometown or places you plan on visiting for business and pleasure.

160

restaurant guides

Where to eat no matter where you are

Online restaurant guides serve up the reviews. They also help steer you to a memorable meal by letting you sort locations by cuisine, neighborhood, or price range. They'll also tell you when reservations are a must, so you can call in advance to ensure you taste the feast that you desire. Although there are numerous regional gastronomic guides, three of the best national directories include:

www.zagat.com—The online version of the Zagat guides is as opinionated as the original little books that now cover most major metropolitan areas. That's because the same reviews fill both the printed guides and this Web site. You don't have to pay for the online version, but you do have to fill out a free registration.

www.cuisinenet.com—Turn here to get a second opinion on a restaurant that sounded promising at Zagat. It lets you quickly sort by cuisine or neighborhood to track down a best bet.

www.dine.com—A major advantage of the reviews on this site is that you can see how different reviewers rated various restaurants. You get to judge the judgers. If they seem to have well-founded reasons for going to one restaurant and avoiding another, you can check out their recommendations for the best places to eat. One drawback to **Dine.com**: Although it claims to review 125,000 restaurants, the site's coverage lacks strength in the Northeast outside of Boston. Still, it's a great source of information on what types of restaurants exist in smaller towns across the U.S.

international guides

Time spent on the Web helps you look like a local

Whether you prefer hauling your backpack between hostels or camping out at a local Hilton, you should head to the Web before making major decisions about an international holiday. Here are some online sites for overseas information:

www.lonelyplanet.com—For tracking down details about out-of-the-way locales or traditional tourist destinations, the Lonely Planet series has gained growing admiration. Some may be put off by the overtly leftish political viewpoints, but the site provides plenty of useful information along with the sermons.

www.fodors.com—The "dad" of the online travel guides doesn't cover as many locations as its younger competitors. You can browse through the entire archive of more than 100 cities worldwide. Fodor's can paste together a tailored Web page just for you that includes only the travel information you want to put in.

www.roughguides.com—It exudes the self-confidence of the twenty-something crowd to which the British guidebooks cater. The online guides come straight from the book series and win you over with detailed history about each of the countries, cities, and regions profiled.

FIRST PERSON DISASTER

Listen Up

I hadn't done anything fancy with our computer except e-mail friends and family. Then a friend told me there was a Web site that could help me plan a trip my wife and I were taking to France. There was even a feature that would teach you everyday expressions. I found the site and sure enough it had tons of useful information. Then I clicked on Everyday Expressions in French. The words were there but no sound. I figured I needed speakers so I went to our local computer store and got audio speakers and set them up. I clicked on the Web site. Still no sound. When we went to France, I tried using my newfound French. But when I asked at a newstand to buy a magazine, I got yelled at. When I told our hotel manager about it, he corrected my pronunciation. Store and magazine are similar words, but pronounced differently. I was asking to buy the store, instead of a magazine. A week after we were home, my wife asked why I had gotten new speakers for the computer when they were already built in. Oh, and by the way, did I know she had turned off the sound because she didn't like the beeps it made? I quietly asked her how to turn the sound back on.

Anthony S., Sarasota, Florida

HAT IF

You need to know visa restrictions for various countries?

All of the online guides tell you whether or not you need to acquire a visa from a country's embassy or consulate. Most foreign governments also have tourism bureaus on the Web that can help you find out where to write for a visa.

You want information on a country in its native language?

Nearly all Web sites use English as their default language. If you want to hear about a country in its native tongue, you can look for sites that use the actual language. Click on **www.american express.com** and choose the country's flag to hear it spoken about in its native language. If you want to have a simple phrase translated, click on **www.travlang.com**.

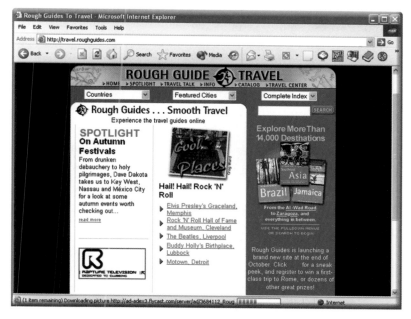

The online versions of popular guidebooks allow you to plan an overseas trip without buying the book—although you'll want the paper version to throw in your travel bag.

CITIZEN ALERT

When you travel overseas, it's always a good idea to keep an eye on the news. But no publication—not even *The New York Times*—tracks every epidemic or riot in some obscure corner of the globe. The U.S. State Department does better than most, partly because its job is to keep Americans aware of potential problems. You can view its up-to-date alerts about traveling to specific countries at **www.state.gov** by clicking on the services icon and linking to Travel Warnings.

now what do I do?

Answers to common problems

Can I get maps outside the mainland United States?

Yes, but they are not plentiful. Nearly all travel software publishers have Web sites where they list all the maps included in their software packages. Check and see if they have international maps. Most map Web sites have some international maps. Keep hunting around the Web for newly added maps.

Do any of the programs tell you about bridge and road tolls?

Most of the Web sites do not tell you about tolls, but the software generally does. In fact, some of the Web sites won't even tell you that you'll be crossing a bridge in your travels.

What if I want to take an alternate route or make a few diversions?

Just enter the alternate route into the trip-planning software when you enter your destination. Or you can either highlight the new route with your mouse or just drag and drop the originally mapped-out route to a new route. For most of the trip-planning programs and the Web sites you can add different routes—say, past national monuments or to avoid inner-city gridlock—just by adding more information.

Can I calculate my car's gas mileage?

Using your route-planning software, figure out how much of the journey is highway driving, and how much is local stop-start city driving. Then go to the Energy Department's Web site (**www.fueleconomy.gov**), enter your car's year and model. You can customize their annual gas costs by hitting the Customize link, and entering the length of your trip, the breakdown of highway versus city driving, and the price of gas in your area. Bingo! Your gas mileage and pretty accurate costs.

Can I zoom in on local streets?

Yes, you can zoom from the entire United States down to local roads with a few mouse clicks. In several of the trip-planning programs you can control the amount of detail on your maps. Not interested in local roads? Take them out. Want to see every possible type of road from major interstate highways to side streets? Make the map as detailed as possible.

Can I book a hotel room from the software programs?

Not exactly, but many of the programs and all of the trip-planning Web sites have business deals with national hotel chains, so you can go to the hotel's Web site for rates, specials, and lodging information.

Can I see buildings and other man-made structures on the maps for landmarks?

No. The trip-planning programs are like standard road maps; that is, you only see roads, city and county lines, and the outline of parks. Usually, pushpins mark the street address of an establishment.

What if I want to go camping?

The Web contains a wealth of information about parks and regions. The National Park Service details all the national parks at its site (**www.nps.gov**). Most state and local parks departments include similar information about the preserves that they oversee. If you already know what region you'll be visiting, you can guide yourself from state to local area in Yahoo! (look under the Regional heading for the U.S. States link). They'll help you find towns where you can stock up on groceries (or spend a night before heading out) near parks you'll be visiting.

Why isn't the guide in English?

Just about every destination attracts native-speaking tourists, but overseas sites also want to attract foreigners (that's you), so they produce two versions of the site, one that's in English and one that's in the native tongue. Look for an American or British flag. Click on it, and you'll find the English version of the tourist information you're after.

HELPFUL RESOURCES

CONTACTS	BOOKS
Tourism Offices Worldwide www.towd.com	**Travel Planning Online for Dummies** By Noah Vadui and Julie Smith
National Parks www.nps.gov	

e-Fun & games

9

Your computer is an instant party waiting to happen. In this chapter there are Web sites where you can play games, to say nothing of the many fabulous computer games you can buy. Fun for kids from 1 to 92.

fun software

Try out a computer game and join the fantastic new world of virtual fun

True, your computer will help you accomplish many important goals in your daily life: filing taxes, e-mailing family and friends, writing the local community newsletter. But there are many completely frivolous and wildly fun things to do—like play computer games.

There are all kinds of games/entertainment software out there for all age groups. By now you'll already have sampled the delights of Windows' built-in card games—Solitaire, Hearts, and FreeCell (if not, see pages 26–27). Get ready for some serious fun: There are also sports simulations, puzzles, learning games, and quest games.

Where do you get these games? You buy them at computer stores or electronics stores. Some require only one CD-ROM disk that you load in your CD-ROM drive (see page 24) and then can store permanently on your hard drive. Others come with several CD-ROMs because they are so full of music and animated action that everything can't fit on one CD-ROM. Moreover, you shouldn't install them on your hard drive, because all those CD-ROMs would use up your computer's memory. This just means that to play games that require more than one CD-ROM, you'll need to change disks to continue playing.

ASK THE EXPERTS

I just bought a games software package, and it includes a $20 mail-in rebate offer. Is it worth sending it in?

Rebate offers are a hassle, but consumers who go to the trouble of filling out the forms and mailing them in can expect to get their rebate checks within six to eight weeks.

What's a joystick, and how will it improve my game play?

If you feel that the arrow keys on your keyboard or your mouse don't give you the control you want when you're driving a virtual race car or controlling a plane on a flight simulator, you might want to treat yourself to a separate game controller. **Game controllers**, also known as joysticks (they're shaped like a handle that moves around on a base, to let you control your character's or your vehicle's movements), are made by companies including Gravis and Microsoft, and are available for under $100.

Why are the images in my CD game jumpy?

You may need to upgrade your graphics card. Most PCs today come with 16 MB of video **RAM,** or memory, enough to accommodate the intense graphics of most computer games. But if your computer is more than a couple of years old, chances are you have less than 16 MB of video RAM. If that's the case, companies including Diamond Multimedia and Creative Labs sell individual upgrade cards for about $150. Some new games require a 3-D video card, which costs $150. If reading this is bringing on an anxiety attack, call a techie friend who can help you, or ask your local computer store to help you buy and insert the card.

games software

Board games, card games— you name it, it's available on the computer

If you're into classic board or card games—look no further than your computer store's software shelf. You can find cool animated versions of dozens of card games—as well as board games like chess and even Monopoly.

Most of the classic games have been packaged by Sierra into several popular collections such as—*Hoyle Word Games*, *Hoyle Card Games*, and *Hoyle Board Games*. Amid names you'll recognize, like Crazy Eights, are some that don't look so familiar, but you'll know the games. For copyright reasons Sierra couldn't use names like Scrabble or Parcheesi, but they include play-alikes under names like Double Cross and Pachisi. With these game collections you pick a game and an animated character who will represent you in the game. You then pick your opponents—a motley collection of adversaries with different skill levels—by clicking on names in a list. Then you use the mouse to roll dice, move pieces, or handle cards. Otherwise the play is just like the real thing. Except for one thing: If your opponents' strongly defined personalities get on your nerves, you may want to turn off the sound to mute them.

One of the PC's most venerable and popular games is MindScape's Chessmaster—which is now up to version 8000, though older versions are still knocking around. The Chessmaster acts as a worthy opponent who plays at just the right level to keep you on your toes— while you use the mouse to shift three-dimensional pieces around a virtual board. Check it out.

ASK THE EXPERTS

Do I need another keyboard to play against someone else?

No. If you're playing a two-player game and want to sit next to someone to play it, you can go through menus in your software to set up one keyboard for two players. Or one of you might use the arrow keys while the other uses a mouse.

My computer game just froze. Now what do I do?

Occasionally, your computer will "lock up," or "hang," while processing the large amounts of data found on computer games. If this happens, take your hands off the keys and wait a few moments to see if the program rights itself. If it doesn't, simultaneously press the Ctrl, Alt, and Delete keys found at the bottom of your keyboard. This will give you the option of closing down the program. Highlight the name of the troublesome program and click End Task, then restart by clicking on the game at your Start menu.

FIRST PERSON DISASTER

Game Called Off

I was starting to feel pretty good at using my PC. I could e-mail and surf the Web. Then I saw this neat-looking software game with 3-D action at the computer store. It would be perfect for my six-year-old nephew who was coming to visit for the weekend. I though I'd test it out and loaded it in my PC. I double-clicked on the icon and a dialogue box popped up that said I needed a 3-D accelerator card to run the program. What?! I called the computer store and asked them what to do. Turns out I had bought a game that required a 3-D accelerator video card which controls the games graphics so it looks like 3-D. The card is standard with most new computers. My PC—purchased only a year ago—didn't have one. If I had read the system requirements at the bottom of the box, I would have seen that it required the 3-D accelerator card. The store said that I could buy the card and get it installed, but it would cost about $100. No thanks. Naturally, because I had opened the software package, I couldn't return it.

Laura W., Dayton, Ohio

cool games

Get ready to be dazzled, challenged, knocked off your block . . .

Fortunately for us, those computer-game programmers didn't just sit around and make imitations of games you know and love. Oh, no, they took the amazing graphic power of the computer and along with its tremendous memory created a whole new generation of games that are astounding.

Take *SimCity*, for example. Maxis (of Electronics Arts) generated this game more than a decade ago, and it's been a huge favorite ever since. SimCity is a simulation game, but instead of simulating a sport or a board game, it simulates an entire city. You act as a city's founding father and city planner and mayor—and watch as the city evolves over the decades. At the start of the game you pick a location and build anything you want upon it—aqueducts, landscaping, factories, houses, and apartment buildings—by dragging each item into place onto your town. Then you wait. *SimCity* will calculate how many people will move to your city, based on the kinds of employment, housing, and education you have provided.

You click to set the time line—maybe five years will pass, and perhaps the population declines. If that happens, your city loses funds from its tax base, and you can't afford to build bigger roads or more schools. (Yes, it does get this realistic!) Sometimes a natural

To build your own city, click and drag on the various building items shown on the tool bar. Beware—your choices will either positively or negatively impact the development of your city as it moves through the time line.

disaster will strike, and then you need to figure out how to save your city infrastructure. Sometimes you'll realize you need better schools to attract more workers to your city. Sometimes your place becomes a ghost town, and you need to start again.

It's heady stuff, but it's so well designed that variations of *SimCity* are used to train people considering a career in government or other public service. And you can even play an early, simple version of the game at **www.simcity.com**—or just watch other people's cities to get an idea of how the game goes.

Another building type of game is Hasbro Interactive's *Tetris*. This compelling game started out as a Russian engineer's experiment in PC programming in the mid-1980s and has been a top-selling game ever since. It's a simple but addicting game for one player (though it's fun to vie for the high score against other people). In it, shapes fall down slowly from the top of the screen, and you use the arrow keys to make them pile up tidily at the bottom. The shapes vary from lines to squares to Z shapes, but if you rotate and pile them properly, you can fill up a straight line across the bottom of the screen, which makes the layer of shapes disappear. Your goal is to prevent the shapes from piling up to the top of the screen.

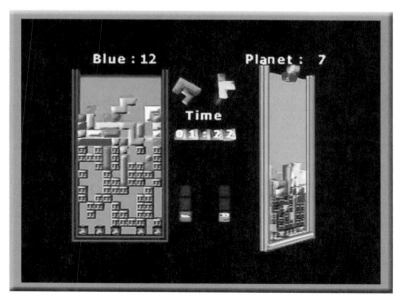

There are several different versions of **Tetris** for the PC including **Tetris Gold**, **Super Tetris**, and the recently released **The Next Tetris**. They all have basically the same game play, and as you get good at each game, the game gets progressively faster.

more cool games

Ready to be completely challenged?

Want to try your hand at games that are both beautiful and mind-boggling? Then take a crack at *Myst* and *Riven*, two games that combine strange landscapes, pleasant ambient music, and almost no instructions!

Myst came first, and *Riven* is its sequel. In both, when you pop the CD-ROM into its drive and start up the game, you're looking at a landscape with strange features (Is it on another planet? Is that a spaceship? Some strange building? You simply don't know at the beginning). You use your mouse to point the way you want to explore. You'll come across artifacts and writing you don't understand, but they all fall together in a cohesive plot when you figure it all out.

Although these are true computer games, you'll need to take some notes to crack the story line. You have to provide the pen, but its software maker provides plenty of pages in a real notebook they include along with the CD-ROM.

Still don't understand what these games are about? Well, the real fun in both is to figure it out for yourself. You become immersed in the world of *Myst*, and if anyone tells you exactly what's going on, you probably won't thank them for it in the long run. So set some time aside—make it a whole weekend—and get lost in one of these games. And when you've figured it out, don't give away the secrets to whoever plays it after you. Just drop the occasional hint, and watch them puzzle it out.

In both **Myst** (top) and **Riven** (bottom), the quest is to find a missing object and uncover the story behind it. To move through the game, click on any item, for example, the telescope, to see what it can reveal.

kids' game software

Here's why today's child is more computer literate than his parents

Don't be fooled by the video arcades or those loud TV ads. Children's computer games, while they look slick and well-scripted, are actually interactive reasoning games that develop a child's deductive powers. For fun and games—with a little bit of a challenge—there's no shortage of CD-ROM games for preschool through grade school years. All kids' game software has an age range printed in big type on the box—generally a spread of three or four years—so you'll know what level to pick.

Humongous Entertainment dominates the cartoon exploration game scene for this age group. Its cartoon characters—Putt-Putt the purple car, Pajama Sam, the boy who thinks he's a superhero, Freddi Fish, and Spy Fox—each stars in a series of several games called *Junior Adventures*. Each game works in pretty much the same way. Your kid sits and watches a cartoon-style introduction that sets up the story. Each story has a quest element—in *Putt-Putt Saves the Zoo* you must find lost animals in time for the zoo's grand opening, for example—and your child has to find the way to save the day. To move around the place, they point the mouse toward any side of the screen. If that's a direction you can move, the mouse pointer turns into a big arrow. Click on it, and you direct the action that way. There are plenty of characters and challenges to meet, so players need to keep their eyes open for things that might help along the way. You need to click on objects to pick them up—you never know when a purple sea anemone or a mug of cocoa will help you get past an obstacle.

ASK THE EXPERTS

How early should a child start on the computer?

Most experts say age three, but it depends on your child. Bear in mind your child needs to have some fine motor-skill development to be able to handle the mouse successfully. The key is to monitor your child's enjoyment of the computer; if he gets frustrated, move on to something else, like a book or a noncomputer game.

I can't afford a CD-ROM game right now. How can I keep everyone entertained on the PC?

There are plenty of Web sites that feature interactive games you can try out for free. At Headbone Interactive (**www.headbone.com**) there are lots of games for preteens. Or visit Nickelodeon's site (**www.nickjr.com**) for activities based on favorite characters from *Blue's Clues* and the *Busy World of Richard Scarry*. For more online games, go to Yahoo Games (**games.yahoo.com**) and click on any game that interests your child.

In **Putt-Putt Saves the Zoo**, the pointer turns into a big arrow, so when you click on any part of the screen, that's where Putt-Putt (the little purple car) will go. You can also click on various items, such as a newspaper or oil can, and they will appear in the dash-board to be used to solve problems later in the game.

kids' learning software

Educational computer games are fun

For preschoolers there's a host of friendly character-based software. Reader Rabbit is one of the more venerable characters in the digital world. He's the star of a series of programs that start teaching the very young (ages 18 months and up) basic computer, math, and language skills—and ends up in school-age titles teaching them third-grade math. Knowledge Adventures' *JumpStart Toddlers, JumpStart Preschool,* and *JumpStart Spanish* cover the same territory, with pictures that you click on to visit games, painting, and click and drag building activities. For the very young, *Toddlers* greets players with a friendly Giggles the Gopher, a character who points out seven "hot spots" that kids can click on to visit activity areas.

For grade school children the educational titles get a bit more challenging. These software "games" are designed to complement what kids are learning in the classroom. The JumpStart and Reader Rabbit titles—and Humongous Entertainment's Big Thinkers too—provide

JumpStart Spanish teaches vocabulary by having the child click on an item to hear and see the Spanish word.

grade-based general activities. And there are titles geared to specific subjects too, to give a boost in areas where a child may be flagging— such as *JumpStart Phonics Learning System* or *Reader Rabbit's Math Ages 6-9*. To get a good overview of appropriate titles, check out the reviews at **www.gamespot.com** and click the "Reviews" button.

SK THE EXPERTS

Can my child stop halfway through a program?

It's possible to get through a Junior Adventure title in a few hours, but that's too long for a little one to sit still. So you can press your keyboard's S key to save a game (the screen you're at will appear in a little photo album), and when you start the game up again, you press L (for load) and click on the scene you just left to pick up where you left off. The Junior Adventures are very well scripted and funny, so that they can keep even boisterous preteens entertained (though they're aimed at 3- to 10-year-olds).

How do I help my child stay motivated to learn on these computer learning games?

Each of the reading and math titles in the Reader Rabbit series features a section where parents can create and print award certificates. These colorful, authentic-looking "achievement" certificates will help keep your child motivated to go to the next level. They also make nice wall decorations!

How realistic is it to expect my child and his friends to play on the computer together peacefully?

Actually, many educational software titles for children encourage them to yell out answers, sing along, and play games with the characters on the screen. All of this can be done with multiple players.

now what do I do?

Answers to common problems

I'm trying to play an old computer game I got from my cousin, but it won't start up. A box comes up saying I need 256 colors. What does that mean?

Your monitor, like most computer monitors these days, is probably running what's called 16-bit High Color. This means that your screen can display thousands of colors—so that digital photographs, for example, will look good. Some older games are designed to run in only one "color mode"—usually the lowest common denominator, 256 colors. But you can easily change your display, so don't worry. Right-click on a blank spot on the Windows desktop. On the menu that appears, click on Properties. In the Display Properties box that appears, click on the Settings tab. At the bottom left you'll see a color bar and a little drop-down list with your various color options—most computers will have 16 colors, 256 colors, High Color and True Color. Pick the one your game wants, click on OK, and get ready to play.

How can I tell whether my computer can actually run a game I see in the store?

All computer games have a set of minimum system requirements—that is, a listing on the box that shows what your computer should have to run the game. If you want to run the game, make sure your computer matches (or preferably exceeds) all the requirements in the box. A lot of games are designed to run on both Windows PCs and Macintosh computers, so be sure to check out the Windows PC requirements. Before you go shopping, make a note of your computer's details. These are the ones to look out for:

The system requirements will include the **processor** or CPU (usually a Pentium or Pentium II, or perhaps a 486). You'll also see a processor speed number—maybe 133Mhz or 266Mhz. You'll know whether you have this kind of processor from your computer's documentation or your invoice.

You'll also see an **operating system** requirement—Windows 95, 98, ME, or XP. Some games even list Windows 3.1—a much older operating system. Don't worry if your version of Windows is higher than the version listed on the box—a Windows 3.1 game will run under Windows 98.

You'll also see a **RAM** (Random Access Memory) or memory requirement—maybe 32MB. If you don't know how much RAM your system has, right-click on My Computer and select Properties from the menu. In the System Properties box you'll see the amount of RAM installed in your PC.

The other important requirement is your screen properties—you may need 800-by-600 resolution and 16-bit color. Don't let these numbers intimidate you! You can find out these numbers by right-clicking on a blank bit of your Windows desktop and clicking on Properties. Click on the Settings tab near the top right of the box. Now look at the Colors and Screen Area figures. Note the current setting of Colors and click on the little down-arrow triangle next to it to see whether there's a higher number available. Then make a note of the Screen Area number—maybe 1024 by 768 pixels. If the slider bar is at the far right, near the word More, that's the maximum screen area (or resolution) your computer can handle.

Armed with these details, you're ready to go shopping! And remember, most stores will only take back software that's unopened! So don't buy something you can't run.

I know where I can find movie reviews and book reviews, but where do I find unbiased reviews of computer games?
On the Web, of course! Lots of magazine publishers keep their game reviews online, where you can get an idea of what you'll get if you buy the games and how they rate. A good Web site for grownup games is **www.gamespot.com.**

If you're buying for children, read all about it at the Fun and Games section at Family PC's Web site. Or look for reviews at KB Kids (**www.kbkids.com**)—a site that sells software, but also provides impartial reviews of most of the titles it sells.

(H)ELPFUL RESOURCES

CONTACTS	BOOKS
ZDNet www.gamespot.com	**Great Software for Kids and Parents (The Dummies Guide to Family Computing)** By Cathy Miranter
Hasbro email.games.com	
Yahoo! games.yahoo.com	

glossary

Active window Even when you have lots of different windows open, you can only work on one at a time. It's called the active window, and you can tell which it is by looking at the title bar—on the active window, it will be brightly colored, and the others will be fainter. If you click on a different window, it will become the active one.

Application This is a techie word for a computer program (as distinct from other types of software, like an operating system such as Windows). All the programs you run by clicking icons—Microsoft Word, Excel, Paint, and so on—are applications. But most people just call them "programs"—and we recommend you do too.

Arrow key On a keyboard there are four arrow keys to the right of the letters. They point up, down, left, and right, and are used to move the cursor inside a window.

Alt key On either side of your keyboard's space bar is an Alt key. Press once, and you activate the menu bar. The Alt key can also be used in combination with other keys.

Bit A bit is the smallest amount of information a computer can handle. You'll see it used most often to describe the depth or quality of information—24-bit color, 16-bit sound, and so on. The higher the number you see, the better the quality—and the larger the size of the files!

Browser A program used to view (and hear) the information on the World Wide Web, for example, Netscape Navigator or Microsoft Internet Explorer.

Byte A byte is the basic unit of storage on your computer. It's so small that most of the files you'll see are measured in thousands of bytes (kilobytes, or KB) or millions of bytes (megabytes or MB). Most hard disks these days can hold thousands of millions of bytes, or gigabytes (GB).

CD-ROM They look like regular CDs, but CD-ROMs contain computer data, not just audio tracks.

Chat On a computer, chat doesn't involve your voice at all. It's a typed conversation between two or more people, all of whom are online at the same time. Chats can take place in chatroom sites or using a program like AOL's Instant Messenger.

Click On a mouse, you click by quickly pressing and releasing the mouse button. It's usually done to the left mouse button, but occasionally you'll be called upon to use the right button—this is called a right-click. A double-click is two clicks in swift succession.

Clipboard An out-of-the-way place where Windows puts the last item that you cut or copied. The item always stays hidden, as does the clipboard, in your computer's memory until you select the paste command and paste the item into a document.

Control key On either side of your keyboard's space bar and Window keys is a key labeled either Ctrl or Control. These Control keys, like the Alt key, can also be used in combination with other keys to provide a shortcut to features in Windows. (You hold down Ctrl and press C, for example, to copy an item to the clipboard.)

Control Panel This is the place where you adjust Windows features such as Time, Date, and Remove programs. There are a few ways to get to the Control Panel—either by clicking Start and selecting Control Panel, or double-clicking on My Computer, and double-clicking on the Control Panel icon there.

Copy-and-paste If you need a piece of text or a picture in more than one file, or in more than one place, you can copy it in two steps. First, you copy it to the clipboard (by selecting the Edit menu's copy command, or holding down the Control key and pressing C). From the clipboard, you can create an exact duplicate of whatever you copied as many times as you like, by selecting Edit, Paste or holding down the Control key and pressing V.

Cursor Moving the mouse on your desk surface moves a little picture on your computer screen; that picture is the cursor. It usually looks like an arrow, but sometimes it's shaped like an hourglass or the letter I.

Cut-and-paste If you need to move a piece of text or a picture, you first cut it (by selecting the Edit menu's Cut command, or holding down the Control key and pressing X). From the clipboard, you can create an exact duplicate of whatever you cut as many times as you like, by selecting Edit, Paste or holding down the Control key and pressing V.

Delete key Press it to delete any highlighted items in a file, or to delete letters to the right of the cursor.

Desktop In Windows, the Desktop is everything you see on the screen before you open any programs or folders. It consists of the My Computer and other icons, and any wallpaper pictures you may have.

Dialogue box Any box that appears and asks you to click on a button or enter a word is called a dialogue box. It's called that because Windows wants you to respond in some way—like two people talking.

Disk (floppy) Also called diskettes, floppy disks are the 3½ inch square things that you slip in and out of the slot in your computer. Indeed, they don't look like floppy disks—but underneath that plastic casing there are circles made of flexible Mylar.

Disk format Before a computer disk can be used, it needs to be formatted. Formatting simply magnetizes the right parts of the disk so that when you want to copy programs or files, the computer knows where to put them. Just beware that when you format a floppy disk, you will erase everything that's already on it.

Disk (hard) All the programs and files on your computer are stored on a hard disk, also called a hard drive. It's installed in your PC, so you'll never see it.

Double-click When you're asked to double-click on something in Windows, you move the mouse until the cursor is over the object, and you click the left mouse button twice in quick succession.

Download To copy a file from the Internet onto your home computer.

Drag To drag means to hold down a mouse button and move the mouse. This action causes whatever's under the cursor on-screen to move or become highlighted.

E-Mail Typed messages that are delivered from one computer to another over the Internet.

Explorer Microsoft really likes the word Explorer—so much so they used it to name Windows' file manager and its Web browser. Windows Explorer is the program that shows you the names and icons of files and programs when you click on My Computer and other folders. And Internet Explorer is the program that shows you Web pages when you go online.

Extension All Windows files have a file name and a file extension. The extension is up to three characters long and is listed after the file name and a period. For example, a Word file might be named myPC.doc, where doc is the file extension. Most of the time, you don't even see the file extension—Windows Explorer conceals most of them.

File All the information you see on a computer, and all the programs you run, are stored in files.

File format Because a computer file can contain programs, pictures, text, or sounds, each type of information is stored in a different way. This is called the file format, and it's usually referred to by its file extension. A Microsoft Word file could be in DOC (Document) or RTF format (Rich Text Format), and a picture from the Internet may be in GIF or JPEG format, for example.

Folder In Windows, as in a regular office, files are stored in folders. Using Windows Explorer, you'll see little manila folder icons tucked away in most drives. Double-click on them, and they will open up to reveal the files inside.

Font The style and size of the text you see in a computer is called the font. In a word processing program, you'll see font names like Times New Roman or Arial, and font sizes such as 10 point or 12 point. There are also font styles like Bold and Italic.

Format See Disk format or File format

Icon Little pictures appear frequently in Windows. The ones that do something when you click on them are called icons because they are pictures that represent an action or file.

Internet A massive network of computers that stretches across the whole world.

Menu At the top of almost every Windows program are words like File, Edit, and Help. These are menu headings. Click on them and the menu itself pops down, with options such as Open, Save, and Exit.

Menu bar The place in a program where the menu options are located. In Windows the menu bar is located at the top of your screen.

My Computer The mother of all icons on the Windows Desktop is My Computer. Double-click on it to explore all the disk drives, as well as printer and dial-up networking options.

Paste The second half of a cut-and-paste or copy-and-paste operation, pasting places a copy of whatever is in the Windows clipboard into the file you're working in.

Pixel This cute word is a sort of short version of the two words "picture element," and it refers to the dots that make up a picture. Like the dots that make up newspaper pictures (which you can see clearly using a strong magnifying glass), your computer screen, printouts, and graphics files are all made up of thousands of pixels. (See also Resolution)

Properties Like most computer words with lots of syllables, properties sounds more complicated than it really is. Every file and program in Windows has a Properties box; you simply right-click on its icon and select Properties to view it. There you'll see the file's date, size, and other details about it.

Reset button Your computer has an On/Off button at the front—but most have another button too—the reset button. This one doesn't turn the computer off, but it restarts Windows. Don't press this button unless Windows stops working!

Resolution Resolution has nothing to do with making New Year's promises. In computers, resolution talks about the number of dots, or pixels, in a picture, screen, or printout. (PPI stands for Pixels Per Inch; DPI for Dots Per Inch.)

Right-click There are two or more buttons on a PC's mouse. When you're asked to right-click, you simply click on the button on the right side.

Start button The Start button is the rectangle with a little Windows flag on it that you click on to start all the programs in Windows, and also to start the Windows shutdown process.

System Techies love to bandy the word "system" about—and it can mean several things, so you have to figure it out in the context in which it's used. A system can mean your computer hardware, it can mean the operating software (that is, Windows). And it can mean Windows and the hardware together. Yes, that's right—it's a way techie people can be vague about something while still sounding smart.

Task bar The gray strip at the bottom of the desktop that contains the Start button and the icons of programs that are running.

Title bar The title bar is the top part of a window. At the left it contains the name and icon of the program, and at the right, three buttons that you use to minimize, maximize, or close the window.

Tool bar A bar with buttons or icons. Used to set graphic functions such as changing fonts and type size.

Tray In the gray strip that appears at the bottom of most Windows screens (the task bar) there are two permanent features—a Start button at one end, and at the other, the tray. It earned the name tray because it's recessed and full of interesting goodies—such as a digital clock and the icons of various programs like Volume control.

Upload To send a file from your home computer to the Internet.

VGA You'll often hear techies talking about monitors being VGA or Super VGA. It stands for video graphics array, and VGA means that the screen displays 640 pixels across by 480 pixels down. Super VGA shows more pixels—either 800 by 600 or 1024 by 768. This is just another way of talking about the screen's resolution, so don't let the abbreviation intimidate you.

Volume control Many models of PC have a volume control on the keyboard or speakers—but not every PC maker goes to this trouble. Windows provides its own way of making sounds softer or louder (or muting them altogether). The volume control is hidden behind the loudspeaker icon next to the clock at the other side of the task bar from the Start button. Click once on it to see a slider control and a checkbox you can click in to mute the sound completely.

Web (a.k.a. World Wide Web) The Web is part of the Internet. It contains most of the sites, sounds, and pictures that you want to visit.

Window In Microsoft Windows a window is any box that contains icons and a title bar.

Window key On your keyboard there are two window keys, one on either side of the space bar, next to the Alt keys. Pressing the window key makes the Start menu pop up from the Start key. (The key on the right between the Window Key and Ctrl is called the Program key. Don't worry about it, it's rarely used.)

Wizard Harry Potter fans, relax. In Windows, a Wizard is the name given to a program that takes you through a tough process step by step. At some point, you'll probably see the New Hardware Wizard, the Internet Connection Wizard, and a Help Wizard.

Zoom In a graphics program such as Windows Paint the zoom function does what the zoom lens on a camera does—it takes you closer in to the action. In almost every graphics program you get to zoom by clicking on a magnifying-glass icon and then clicking on the part of the screen you want to see in close-up.

index

THE AUTHOR: UP CLOSE

Matthew James is the pseudonym of a professional computer-technology writer who, after much coaxing, agreed to come down from his technological mountaintop to help real people understand how to use a computer. To do this he agreed to keep his explanations simple and clear-cut and to write in plain English. James has written for some of the most esteemed high-tech publications, including *PC World*, *Computers Made Easy*, *CNET*, and *ComputerUser*. James reminds us that "while the computer is not your friend, if you can tell it what to do, it will do as it is told."

Barbara J. Morgan Publisher, Silver Lining Books

I'm turning on my PC, Now What?! ™

Barb Chintz Editorial Director

Leonard Vigliarolo Design Director

Ann Stewart Picture Research

Della R. Mancuso Production Manager

Marguerite Daniels Editorial Assistant

PICTURE CREDITS

British Library Add. 39943 f.2. 52; **Andrew Chintz** 4, 108; **Karen Copas**, IBM Corporation, Personal Computer Company 9, 10, 11, 14, 17, 28, 33; **Corbis Images** 5, 168;

Richard Lee cover; **Robert Milazzo** 10, 16, 18, 19, 29, 61, 106, 146;

Photo: www.comstock.com 34; **PhotoDisc** 13; **Rubberball Productions** 8;

Sally Mara Sturman 12, 20-21, 49, 58, 79, 86, 91, 120, 136, 147, back cover;

SuperStock 24, 38, 46, 50, 62, 72; **Steven Webster** 7, 37, 57, 83, 97, 113, 131, 145, 167